PRAISE FOR
SOMEDAY MY PRINCE WILL COME

. . .

"Jerramy Fine doesn't need a prince to corner the market on 'charming.'" – JEN LANCASTER, AUTHOR OF *BITTER IS THE NEW BLACK*

"Fine's writing is pithy and funny . . . a fresh twist on the tired tales of offbeat girls in search of their dream." – *USA TODAY*

"Fine's is a charming and humorous story . . . showing that the strength of one's conviction can be the strongest predictor of one's fate." – *PUBLISHERS WEEKLY*

"Inspires readers to believe and go after the impossible, while still trusting in happily ever after." – *HAMPTON'S SOCIAL LIFE*

ALSO BY
JERRAMY FINE

. . .

Someday My Prince Will Come

The Regal Rules for Girls

Bright Young Royals

IN DEFENSE
OF THE
PRINCESS

IN DEFENSE OF THE PRINCESS

How **PLASTIC TIARAS** and **FAIRYTALE DREAMS**
Can Inspire **STRONG, SMART WOMEN**

JERRAMY FINE

author of *Someday My Prince Will Come*

RUNNING PRESS
PHILADELPHIA · LONDON

Books published by Running Press are available at special discounts for
bulk purchases in the United States by corporations, institutions, and other
organizations. For more information, please contact the Special Markets
Department at the Perseus Books Group, 2300 Chestnut Street, Suite 200,
Philadelphia, PA 19103, or call (800) 810-4145, ext. 5000, or e-mail
special.markets@perseusbooks.com.

ISBN 978-0-7624-5877-6
Library of Congress Control Number: 2016930452

E-book ISBN 978-0-7624-5878-3

9 8 7 6 5 4 3 2 1
Digit on the right indicates the number of this printing

Design by Ashley Haag
Typography: Bell South Basic, Bauer Bodoni, and Adobe Caslon

Running Press Book Publishers
2300 Chestnut Street
Philadelphia, PA 19103-4371

Visit us on the web!
www.runningpress.com

For Cecily Guinevere

The eternal feminine draws us upward.

– JOHANN WOLFGANG VON GOETHE

CONTENTS

......

PREFACE

. . . . .

"But I think she might be a real princess!"

"Morgan, honey, just because she has a funny dress on doesn't mean she's a princess. She's a seriously confused woman who's fallen into our laps."

– *ENCHANTED* (2007)

MY MOTHER IS A die-hard feminist. To this very day, she refuses to wear a bra. She sees this as some sort of revolutionary act, insisting that being comfortable is more important than meeting society's expectations about women. Televised beauty pageants were banned in my household because they were seen as glaringly degrading. On the rare occasions when I was allowed to watch something on TV (that wasn't on PBS), I had to mute the commercials so I wouldn't be exposed to all that evil, corporate brainwashing. Anything vaguely capitalistic was the devil; everything that was natural and handmade was revered.

My parents hoped than one day I'd join the Peace Corps, become a human rights lawyer, or develop an organic garden in my local community. But, despite all this hippie parenting, all my mother's staunch feminist views, and all the years of constant encouragement to become a strong, independent woman who would be admired above all for my brain—as a daughter I must have been a terrible disappointment. Because I wanted to be one thing and one thing only: a princess.

I'm not sure when it started. I'm tempted to say that my longing to be a princess began at birth. Is that crazy? All I know is that this noble yearning was so strong there were times in my childhood when I could actually feel it, physically, in my heart.

I may have been only two years old, but I knew that I wanted to live in *a castle*—not a farmhouse decorated with Guatemalan cushions, modern art sculptures, and all kinds of weird antiques. I knew that I belonged in a place with marble floors, sweepings staircases, and four-poster canopy beds, *not* a home with art deco carpeting that my parents found abandoned in an alleyway. I knew I should have been wearing massive crinoline skirts with layers upon layers of petticoats—not homemade outfits of tie-dyed hemp fiber. My backyard may have been filled with tepees and Tibetan prayer flags, but I would close my eyes and imagine vast croquet lawns edged with elegant topiaries and splashing fountains.

You get the picture. But I adamantly believe that my princess cravings were more than a severe case of reverse rebellion. They seemed to stem from something much, much deeper—from a sacred window in my heart that even as a babe in arms I was desperate to open. I felt certain that if only I could fully access that part of me, finally everything would make sense.

When I was five years old, my family moved to a rural farm town in the Rocky Mountains so my parents could get even closer to nature. (Apparently you can never be close enough.) But up until then we lived in Denver—a city filled with a pretty bland collection of architecture. The one exception was the state capitol building, which, compared to the dull structures surrounding it, seemed positively majestic with its polished steps, huge Roman columns, and towering golden dome. The first time I ever saw its stately splendor, I was a toddler strapped into the backseat of the family station wagon. As we drove closer to it and eventually past it, my mom says I had burst into tears. When she asked me what was the matter, I had whimpered simply, "I . . . I . . . didn't see the Queen."

Evidently, I was so upset, she didn't have the heart to tell me that the building wasn't a palace and that the "Queen" didn't live there, or more importantly, that Colorado had no reigning monarchy. I was left to discover these devastating facts on my own, and, for the next few months, every time we drove past the capitol, I would continue to scan the windows anxiously looking for members of the royal family. I harbored a sincere hope that they would recognize me as one of their own, welcome me into the confines of the palace, and rescue me once and for all from my dreadful hippie existence.

"But *where did it come from?*" people ask me—as if wanting to be a princess was some sort of mysterious insect bite.

It's a very good question because I certainly wasn't raised to be a girl who defined myself by whether or not I had a tiara on my head.

"You must have watched lots of Disney movies as a child," they insist, "or read lots of fairy tales?"

Fairy tales? I wish. Since TV wasn't an option, I learned to read before kindergarten and became voracious in my consumption of library books. I loved Nancy Drew and The Baby-Sitters Club, but around third grade, when I started to read the entire Sweet Valley High series, my mother put her foot down and made me read classics like *To Kill a Mockingbird, Great Expectations,* and *The Grapes of Wrath*—all of which were painfully lacking when it came to princessy themes.

Disney movies? You have to remember that this was the late '70s—more than a decade before the likes of *The Little Mermaid* and *Beauty and the Beast* arrived on the scene. Disney Stores simply did not exist—much less entire pink princess aisles filled with mass-market princess merchandise.

Admittedly, my very first outing to the movie theater was to see the original *Snow White and the Seven Dwarfs.* But my parents viewed this rare indulgence as exposure to cinematic history (*Snow White* was the first feature-length cartoon ever made) and a lesson in 1930s animation. My dad is an artist—this stuff was deemed important knowledge to impart to a toddler.

But as I sat in that darkened movie theater, countless frames of hand-drawn dwarfs were the last thing on my mind. Because at last, after nearly three years on planet Earth, I had found someone who truly understood the achings of my heart.

Just like me, Snow White did not belong with her family. Just like me, Snow White was forced to make the most out of living conditions not suited to her royal position. Just like me, Snow White would gaze into the wishing well (or in my case, the fountain at the mall) and dream that someday someone would recognize her inner highness and whisk her off to a kingdom far, far away. From that day forward, I knew I was not alone in the world. And whenever the strict laws of hippiedom became too much for me, I would go to my bedroom, shut the door, and listen to my *Snow White* record on my Fisher Price record player.

My mom claims she would often hear me sobbing, "Snow White, you are *the only one who understands!*"

It doesn't surprise me. To be perfectly honest, I'm not sure if I would have made it through preschool without Snow White's moral support.

A year or so later, my indulgent grandparents, knowing I had no access to normal TV, recorded something for me on their VCR. I'll never forget sitting cross-legged on their living room floor and watching in awe as Diana emerged from her carriage, a vision in billowing taffeta, and began her long walk down the aisle toward her prince. I was speechless. This wasn't just in fairy tales. This wasn't just in Disney movies. This was real. Diana was not a cartoon. She was a living, breathing princess—and I knew with every inch of my soul that I needed to be one too.

So that was it. My career goal was solved at a very early age.

Fast-forward a few decades and you have to give me some credit. No one can say I didn't try. Throughout my childhood I studied everything I could get my hands on about royal protocol, I collected etiquette books, studied royal family trees, subscribed to royal magazines, analyzed royal fashion, kept elaborate scrapbooks on the world's reigning princesses, and eventually wrote several heartfelt letters to Queen Elizabeth's oldest grandson, who just happened to be my age. When it came to my princess passion, if there ever were a time when anyone in my life thought I might "grow out of it"—they quickly realized that they were terribly mistaken.

When I was nineteen, I studied abroad in London where I blissfully immersed myself in endless royal history. When I was twenty-two, I packed my bags and moved to England permanently. I spent my early twenties scouring London's elite nightlife; spending my weekends at Royal Ascot and the Henley Royal Regatta—forever hoping to pin down that elusive prince so at last I might silence my heart.

The royal marriage didn't work out, but I ended up writing a rather amusing memoir about crossing the ocean to pursue this quirky childhood dream. And since its publication, lots of people have pronounced me certifiably insane. I expected that. But something else happened that I did not expect. I was, and continue to be, overwhelmed with letters and e-mails from women all around the world who tell me that they *also want to be a princess*—and who, until they read my book, thought they were the only ones in the entire universe who felt that way.

Not everyone who contacts me has allowed her inner princess to emerge into adulthood as strongly as I have, but the fact remains that there are thousands of women out there who wish that they could be more open about the "strange" princess leanings they have always felt. There are thousands of young women who have led everyone in their lives to believe that they have "grown out of" their princess dream, when in reality they just keep it a secret—for fear of being called silly, immature, antifeminist, or in my case, certifiably insane.

Yet nearly 2 billion people (*a third of the planet!*) felt the need to watch Catherine Middleton walk down the aisle of Westminster Abbey and marry a prince. And yet more than 25,000 distinctive princess products (an industry worth $5 billion) are flying off the shelves at lightning speed.

It seems that regardless of age, education, nationality, socio-economic background, or whatever commercialism, media, and folklore we may or may not have been be exposed to, the idea of a princess continues to capture our hearts. Can we really blame the phenomenon on Disney marketing? On fairytale brainwashing? On rebelling against feminist mothers?

Only partly.

The truth is more simple than that.

The truth is that all women are princesses.

Many don't know it. And some never will. (Royal women aren't always outwardly frilly; in fact, often they are anything but.)

The definition of a princess is simple: she is a queen in the making. A girl with a vision and purpose higher than her own. A girl who understands that being born female is itself a royal power.

Destined to be Queen, a princess is one of the most empowered females in existence—and humanity does not need fewer empowered women; it needs millions more.

Whether it's a Disney princess, a Windsor princess, your daughter's make-believe princess, or your own inner princess—all are worthy. And all need defending.

This book is my case for the princess.

Forever may we reign.

Chapter I

IN DEFENSE OF DISNEY PRINCESSES

. . . . .

"They can't order me to stop dreaming." – CINDERELLA

"You have a library?" – BELLE

I APPROACH EVERY NEW DISNEY princess movie with a mixture of unbridled enthusiasm and mild trepidation. Will it be as good as I know it can be? Will it live up to my sky-high royal standards? Can the Disney Studios of this new millennium compete with the magical films of my childhood?

A few years ago, my brave British husband agreed to go with me to see the newly released *Tangled* (2010) on the big screen (but only if I agreed to go with him to see a movie about a guy who gets stuck in a ravine and cuts off his own arm). We settled down amid the rows of children wearing 3-D glasses, and as the opening scenes unfolded and the narrator told us the story of baby Rapunzel, my heart began to swell.

There is something indescribably moving, almost blissfully spiritual, about those first few Disney moments when you're awash with billowing Alan Menken music and pastel images of royal kingdoms. Even before the teenage Rapunzel appeared on screen, my eyes were welling with tears of happiness. Because I knew for the next one hundred minutes I could allow the sacred princess dream to envelop me completely. Sitting in that darkened theater, I briefly entered a fairytale world—and, just as it had been with *Snow White*, for that small space in time, I was home.

Tangled is based on the classic Grimms' fairy tale Rapunzel, and I've always had a strong affinity for her. This is mainly because my flower-power parents didn't let me cut my hair until fifth grade, and my bohemian tresses reached well below my waist. At school I was a bit of a freak show, but hoping to use my hair as an advantage, I announced that I was tired of being Snow White for Halloween; *this year* I would be Rapunzel.

My always-artsy mother jumped at the challenge (there would be no store-bought costumes in this house!). She found a refrigerator box, spray-painted it silver and drew castle-like stones on the outside before gluing on several vines of silk roses. Finally, she cut an arch-shaped window, out of which I let my long hair tumble while I stood inside.

Safely ensconced in my cardboard tower, I no longer felt like an outcast; I felt regal and I felt powerful. But I also felt that familiar aching that perhaps someone, somewhere, would recognize me—and explain the strange royal yearnings that seemed etched into my soul.

Watching *Tangled* brought all those feelings back again. When Rapunzel recognized the royal symbol on her tower wall and finally realized *who she was*, my heart pounded with an ancient recognition of my own. Rapunzel is a princess who was lost but then found—a notion that embodies the very core of the entire princess genre, a notion with which so many girls, myself included, fiercely identify.

Although early Disney princesses like Snow White and Cinderella are often accused of being too meek and too mild, in this movie, Rapunzel is very much the opposite. With her long hair, bare feet, and obvious talent for wall murals and chalk drawings, I knew from the start that my bohemian parents would *adore* her. But, more than this, Rapunzel is completely unassuming. If you asked her if she wanted a palace and jewels and all that royal prestige, I'm fairly certain she'd say no.

Rather than waiting to be rescued, Rapunzel actually succeeds in rescuing the male lead on more than one occasion. And appearances don't matter to her one bit. She is not remotely attracted to the hero's smoldering looks (she eventually falls for his honesty and kindness), and, when her magical golden hair gets cropped short, she couldn't care less. Yes, she is beautiful, but more than that she is bold, and most of all she is brave. (The name Rapunzel is actually derived from the botanical Latin for *Rapunculus*, a beautiful plant known to survive in harsh conditions.)

As my husband and I sat in a Thai restaurant later that evening, I tried to describe to him the inexplicable "high" I experienced while watching *Tangled* (and all other princess movies). To his infinite credit, he was able to keep a straight face through most of my gushing. But then he shrugged and said, "I guess that's kind of how I feel when I surf the perfect wave. You become part of something completely indescribable and for those few seconds the world makes sense."

And they say the British aren't in touch with their feelings?

There it was in a nutshell: princess stories, and all they entail, are perfect waves—and it's clear to me that little girls, young and old, all over the world are desperate to surf.

PRINCESSES ARE WOMEN TOO

. . .

LET ME PRE-EMPT YOU and get right to the point: Can loving princesses coexist with everything we hope and want for women of the world? Can loving princesses coexist with everything we hope and want for our daughters? Of courses it can. And it does.

I have to tell you that I definitely didn't set out to write a book that had anything to do with feminism. But as I began to draft the chapters of this book, the topic kept rearing its princessy head. And it suddenly became impossible for me to even mention the word "princess" without someone bringing it up.

It's true that women have endured some form of oppression or injustice for most of human history, and sadly there is no straight-forward solution to fixing this. It's an incredibly complicated and emotional topic, and, let me tell you, when you put a princess nut like me in a room with people who have studied feminism at Harvard, it's not always pretty. But when the last of the wine is poured, we do agree on one thing: however it happens, our ultimate goal is to obtain equal power for women.

It's a very simple goal, and yet it connects all feminists in history—be they suffragettes from the past century, 1960s "bra burners" like my mother, subscribers of *Ms. Magazine*, readers of *Jezebel*, fans of Beyoncé, followers of Lena Dunham, or devotees of Emma Watson. This goal even connects all these feminists with princess nuts like me.

Because you know what? Female empowerment is *also* the fundamental message of the princess. And if viewed this way, we can see that our worldwide princess obsession is not damaging—but actually a healthy, natural, and essential mechanism to help all of us reach the same goal.

My idea of empowerment may not be identical to your idea of empowerment, but even if you disagree with anything or everything that I say, I want you to know that, deep down, *we are on the same side.*

Part of what made me want to write this book was watching how, year after year, the Disney princesses have taken punch after punch in the name of feminism.

At first it was a slow beating. But it's turned into a rather violent thrashing that shows no signs of abating.

"I'd happily blow the brains out of a Disney Princess!" read one recent headline in London's *Telegraph.*[1]

"Disney princesses are the evil disciples that the cult of Disney sends out into the world," continues the columnist, "pretty little hookers . . . turning tricks on the minds of our young."

That's only the beginning. There's a hostile undercurrent within the "princess free" movement that seems to say if a little girl likes princesses, then she can't also be intelligent or independent, or that her mother is obviously ignorant and uninformed about marketing influences. In this way, princess critics often seem just as guilty of making blanket statements about girls and women as the commercial patriarchy they are supposedly fighting against.

As things stand, many believe the genre's single purpose is to instill unrealistic expectations in young girls' minds, and Disney princesses are now getting blamed for everything from bulimia to date rape. Mothers across the country are now questioning themselves, wondering whether letting their daughters play with the likes of Cinderella and Snow White (not to mention Ariel, Belle, or even the girls from *Frozen*), that they are somehow damaging their self-esteem and setting them up to be weak, submissive women. Disney princesses are regularly called helpless, brainless, passive, and superficial—when actually they are anything but.

(I find it maddening when "feminists" fiercely challenge such connotations when they are used to undermine women yet seem to think it's totally fine to use these same labels to undermine princesses.)

The bottom line is that princesses are easy targets because our society dismisses anything feminine as weak or second best. But if we want to stop the oppression of women and the oppression of all things feminine, we must also stop the oppression of the princess dream and all it represents.

So, just as I wouldn't allow any real women to be thrashed in front me, I can't allow these animated women to be bullied any longer.

After all, princesses are women too.

And if no one else is going to stand up for them, I will.

WHERE DOES IT COME FROM?

* * *

AN OLD HIGH SCHOOL friend of mine is what I call a reluctant MOP (mother of a princess)—and, just as my parents did with me, she finds the origin of her daughter's all-consuming princess fascination to be a complete mystery. To the best of my friend's ability, she actively shields her toddler from anything princess-related and refuses to purchase any Disney-branded toys, movies, or merchandise. She shops at independent stores that carry products devoid of princess-themed marketing images, her daughter is enrolled in a Montessori school where commercial images are not allowed on the children's clothing or backpacks, and all of her daughter's playmates have like-minded parents.

"And yet," her baffled mother confides to me, "my daughter can happily name every Disney princess on the face of the earth. She wears her father's socks on her arms and tells us they are princess gloves, she puts on my shoes and insists they are glass slippers, and she has been known to employ everything from a cardboard box to her own underwear as a princess crown. Where did this come from? I honestly have no idea."

There's that eternal question again: Where did it come from?

I tried to explain that the princess dream doesn't exist just because Disney is selling it. That it's actually an ancient archetype that girls subconsciously recognize and subconsciously crave. When our daughters dress in their princess regalia, they are not attempting to be sexual objects or resigning themselves to domestic passivity—they're asserting an ancient feminine force.

My friend stared at me blankly, but I persisted.

You see, children don't resist their greatness like grown-ups do. They know that playing small does not serve the world. Before adults start telling them their dreams are impossible or silly, children tend to dream big. They come into the world knowing that they were born to rule and, with makeshift capes on their shoulders and plastic tiaras on their heads, they have zero shame expressing it. If wearing a Disney princess dress helps their cause, more power to them. Why tell little girls that "good enough" is okay, when they prefer to be exalted?

My friend continued to look at me as if I were a bit bonkers.

"So you mean to tell me this has *nothing* to do with Disney?" she asked skeptically. "Can't you see how they are indoctrinating our children purely for profit?"

I couldn't ignore her point. Is the princess craze making lots of money for Disney? Yes. Absolutely. But there is nothing new about begrudging the forces of advertising aimed at our children. There's nothing new about begrudging the forces of money and marketing in general. We all know that sex is used to sell beer and clowns are used to sell hamburgers and pink is used to sell princesses. If we want to attack the evils of corporate greed and its overall effect on our world, that's a whole other subject (and a whole other book).

Instead, we need to look beyond this and understand that the princess phenomenon is not simply a case of marketing genius gone berserk—it's about recognizing our girls' desire to bring the intrinsic princess archetype to life. So while I told my friend that she was free to vent her frustration with Disney's corporate strategy and their commercial profits, we had to be clear about one thing: my royal girls are blameless.

REGAL ROLE MODELS?

. . .

Professor Amy M. Davis, a scholar after my own heart, embarked on an academic study (that I am actually quite envious of because it sounds so fun), in which she painstakingly analyzed female depictions in all past and present Disney movies as a whole.[2]

After years of research and countless viewings of more than seventy years' worth of Disney footage, Davis concluded that "far from portraying weak, passive females, the Disney Studio has presented an image of women—and femininity—which, although not perfect, is largely positive in its overall make-up."

I could have told her that.

But critics will insist that parents should absolutely not turn to Disney princesses if they are serious about presenting good role models to their girls. In her bestselling book *Cinderella Ate My Daughter*, author Peggy Orenstein asserts that these animated royal women have nothing to offer anyone other than their beauty and melodic sensibilities.[3] (Orenstein does make an exception when she admits that Snow White's lone virtue is "tidiness"—but that's about it.)

I'm not suggesting we negate all critical thinking when it comes to viewing Disney films with our children—but if someone tells me that Disney princesses possess zero redeeming qualities, I must and will protest.

If you look carefully, you'll find that Disney has never actively championed the passive domestication of women—rather they champion female characters who are underdogs, outcasts, or exiles. Admittedly, Disney's earlier movies (*Snow White, Cinderella*, and *Sleeping Beauty*, which were released in 1937, 1950, and 1959, respectively) hail from a historical era when American women played a much more compliant role in society. In this context, it's not surprising that Cinderella, Aurora, and Snow White embody this early American ideal of female deference and sweetness; they were what feminist author Virginia Woolf referred to as "the angel in the house":

. . . intensely sympathetic . . . immensely charming . . . utterly unselfish . . . excelled in the difficult arts of family life . . . sacrificed daily . . . Above all, she was pure.[4]

Not bad qualities, but not particularly liberating either. Still, we must remember that Cinderella, Aurora, and Snow White, even though they are two-dimensional cartoons, suffered the same societal restraints as our grandmothers. But living in a man's world doesn't mean that our grandmothers were weak women. And it certainly doesn't mean they were bad role models. So please keep that in mind before passing any judgment on these erstwhile princesses.

Though the early Disney movies may seem outdated, what's interesting is our modern society clearly believes these particular princess stories are worthy of preservation. If *Snow White, Cinderella,* and *Sleeping Beauty* did not resonate with us on some level, if they did not resonate with our daughters on some level, then despite the best efforts of Disney's marketing departments, they would have faded from popularity long, long ago.

GOOD GIRLS WITH BIG DREAMS

• • •

I ONCE STAYED HOME from fourth grade with a bad case of strep throat. I remember the day clearly because it was the day my dad gave me a book he had found at the Salvation Army (his favorite shopping destination). The book was entitled *The Complete Fairy Tales by Brothers Grimm.*

It was a thick, tattered volume with a fading burgundy cover, a broken spine, and ragged corners, but it also had pages that were *edged in gold.* To me, it seemed a medieval relic. Something that would not have been out of place in the rooms of a seventeenth-century palace. Needless to say, I devoured it.

I did not have the luxury of constantly rewatching my favorite Disney movies on an iPad, DVD player, or even a VCR. But now I could read the text that they were based on over and over again. Of course, I always started with my silly-sounding favorites: *Aschenputtel (Cinderella), Schneewittchen (Snow White), Dornröschen (Little Briar Rose*—the Grimms' version of Perrault's *Sleeping Beauty)*, and then I would move to *The Princess and the Pea* or *The Twelve Dancing Princesses.*

Whispering to the deepest hollows of my heart, those ancient fairy tales got right to the point: Hold on. Hold out. Work hard. You will find your own way.

IN A WORLD HEAVING with male-driven narratives, fairytale princesses—and the classic movies inspired by them—demonstrate to young girls that their stories deserve to be told. (It's worth noting in both *Snow White* and *Cinderella,* the story itself is named after the heroine, while the prince remains nameless throughout!)

Besides, it takes very little deconstruction to find redeeming qualities beneath the retro storylines. For instance, both Snow White and Cinderella make the most of their dreadful situations. Rather than become jaded or cynical (or moping over the more comfortable life that they've lost), these girls stay true to themselves and never lose their inherent kindness.

In *The Curse of the Good Girl*, author Rachel Simmons warns that by idealizing the "good girl" (one that is unerringly kind, selfless, and polite)—we are teaching girls to be cautious, apologetic, and conforming.[5] Apparently by elevating this princessy ideal, we are teaching girls to steer away from taking risks, speaking their minds, or entering any kind of leadership role that might require courage.

I can see where Simmons is coming from; after all, even if girls outperform boys in school, it hardly matters if once they enter the real world they're too afraid to go after what they deserve. Many like to throw the same accusations at Disney princesses because if they aren't classic "good girls," then who is? Yet these royal ladies may surprise you. Because although they are certainly kind and polite, Disney princesses do not conform; they are hardly afraid of speaking their minds, and they have never, ever been afraid to take risks.

No matter which decade or era they hail from, all Disney princesses have one thing in common: the aching need to break free. Although all the princesses are loved (be it by their parents, siblings, dwarfs, mice, or godmothers), they feel trapped in a life that they know in their hearts is not meant for them. Snow White and Aurora are trapped in tiny woodland cottages; Rapunzel is trapped in a tower; Cinderella is trapped in an attic; Ariel feels trapped underwater; Belle feels trapped in her provincial village; and both Jasmine and Elsa feel trapped by the confines of royal duty.

This idea of breaking free is one of the most timeless princess messages in existence. It doesn't matter whether you're four or forty-four, it doesn't matter whether your parents treated you well or treated you terribly—we all experience the same urge to break free and forge a path that is entirely our own.

This basic princess dream speaks directly to the girl who is unpopular at school, the daughter who is an outcast in her family, the wife who is lost in her marriage, and the woman who feels out of place in her religion, her workplace, or her country. This princess dream is so mesmerizing because it speaks to all women. It provides hope in the form of redemption. It is a royal promise that, in spite of life's seeming bleakness, someday, somewhere, someone will truly understand the achings of your heart.

THE RETRO ROYALS

. . .

WE MUST KEEP IN mind that *Snow White and the Seven Dwarfs* was released in 1937—in the middle of the Great Depression and only seventeen years after American women received the right to vote.

Walt Disney remortgaged both his house and his studio to finance the film but I'm so glad he did. Because until *Snow White* came along, *Betty Boop* was the only cartoon series that featured a female in the lead role. (Even Minnie Mouse was there purely to support Mickey.) Yet Snow White took center stage with grace and aplomb.

And so what if tidiness is one of Snow White's greatest skills? More power to her. Society's obsession with office-based careers (and the competitive, materialistic values that often come with them), doesn't automatically appeal to everyone. "Having it all" is a myth because not all women want it all. And as far as I'm concerned, if a modern woman prefers open domesticity (in a thatched cottage full of dwarfs or a suburban home full of children), it hardly means she has failed. We have to stop ridiculing and devaluing women the minute they look after others. And we can start right here, right now, with Snow White.

Besides, if we look beyond all the wishing wells, the washing, and the whistling and look more closely at the real challenges Snow White must overcome through no fault of her own (for starters, her jealous stepmother throws her out of the castle and tries to have her killed), we see that the underlying theme of the story actually deals with the dangers of vanity and how beauty can *hinder* you if you allow it to. (A cautionary tale about beauty? Sounds rather feminist to me.)

Next up we have *Sleeping Beauty*—a movie that, at its worst, exposes young ears to Tchaikovsky. Throughout the film, we watch Aurora wander barefoot through the woods completely uninterested in aristocratic affairs. (She's actually devastated when she learns that she's a princess.)

When I was a little girl, the scene from *Sleeping Beauty* that really hit home with me was during the iconic song "Once upon a Dream."

As Aurora dances through the forest humming about the soul mate she knows is out there, even as a child, I sensed she was touching upon some greater wisdom. Aurora never worried whether her prince would appear one day; she *knew* he would—she knew it because she dreamed it and she trusted her dreams. Her stress-free certainty that someone was out there for her not only taught me about the power of manifestation but brought me much comfort during the tumultuous dating years of my twenties.

And although many assume that the prince does all the rescuing in *Sleeping Beauty* and it's another terrible tale of female passivity, if truth be told, it is the three *female* fairies (Flora, Fauna, and

Merryweather) who are the actual rescuers. (It's worth nothing that long before *Frozen* celebrated female alliances, both Sleeping Beauty and Cinderella relied on female fairies for guidance, support, and assistance.)

In *Sleeping Beauty*, the three fairies break Prince Phillip's chains, lead him out of the dungeon, and constantly clear his path as he rides out to rescue Aurora. The prince would be hopeless without these little ladies, just as the very existence of his character would be irrelevant without Princess Aurora herself.

(And Prince Phillip is not the only guy whose Disney character is defined entirely by a woman. The validity of Prince Charming (both of them!), Aladdin, and Flynn Rider is also directly linked to their successful pursuit of a princess.)

And here's something else that's almost never mentioned: all the Disney princesses (retro and modern) enjoy an extraordinary connection to animals. They chat with birds, dance with owls, and sing with squirrels; they talk to dogs, converse with mice, and confide in horses. As only animals can, these creatures sense the tremendous inner beauty of each princess, and, totally unaware of human concepts like royal rank, they happily devote themselves to serving her—teaching us all how true kindness brings its own power and creates its own kingdoms. It's a simple but quite valuable lesson and its right there, hidden in plain sight.

And since we're on the subject of talking mice, let's move on to Cinderella: the antiprincess brigade's number-one enemy. God knows why this poor girl has become such a reviled figurehead of everything that is wrong about our patriarchal world—for I can think of a lot more who represent a lot worse. All I know is that this princess (who is mourning the loss of both parents and suffering indentured servitude in her own house) is intelligent, empathetic, and brave. She has an incredibly strong sense of self and not once does she let her situation define her.

Cinderella is young but she is wise, and her knowledge that everyone (no matter how cruel) is fighting their own demons allows her to handle the bullying she receives from her stepfamily with tolerance and grace. We observe her cheerful smile and infinite patience; and in spite of all the sadness she's endured, we see how utterly resilient she remains.

As a child, my favorite scene from *Cinderella* was not when she was decked out in her elegant ball gown or riding in her magical coach but when she was dressed in rags and gazing out of her attic window at the glorious castle sparkling in the distance.

I had a postcard of this image when I was in grade school, and for years it hung above my desk as I did my homework—reminding me that, no matter what our circumstances, it's *okay* to dream of something more, to know that you are *worthy* of something more and, rather than downgrade your dreams to fit your reality, you must upgrade your convictions to match your destiny.

Cinderella's worst crime is being brave enough to admit she deserved better. (And politely attending a party to which she was *invited*.) People accuse her of waiting to be rescued, but in reality *she* is the one who defies her horrible situation and does what it takes *to get herself* to the ball.

And Cinderella's opportunity to "escape" was never via the prince but through her decidedly female fairy godmother, a vestige of the goddess archetype and a symbol of all women's potential to transfer their intentions into genuine power. (Many lament the absence of powerful women over fifty in today's media culture—but there she is!)

In 2015, Disney released a new live-action version of Cinderella. It seems that her story is so timeless, her character so enduring, that more than sixty-five years after the original animated film and more than *a thousand* years since her story was first recorded, audiences are still clamoring to see the magical tale of a lowly ash girl who becomes a princess.

IT DIDN'T START WITH DISNEY

. . .

WHAT MANY REFER TO as "classic Disney stories" were actually centuries old before they were put on film. The stories of Sleeping Beauty and Rapunzel can be traced to the Middle Ages with dozens of renditions found throughout all parts of Europe. The tale of Snow White has appeared with little variation everywhere from Ireland to central Africa, and Cinderella can be traced as far back as *ninth-century* China.

When placed in the context of such a considerable span of history and time, the Disney marketing machine becomes largely irrelevant.

"Structurally, fairy tales can be simple," says Neil Gaiman, author of *Stardust*, "but the act of retelling . . . is where the magic occurs."[6]

Fairy tales touch us so deeply that humans have continually cultivated them and passed them down from generation to generation. The most popular have been retold infinite times, adapted from this ancient tradition of oral folklore and eventually printed and reprinted into what we now regard as the classic fairytale canon. And then Disney stepped in and made them part of our present multimedia world.

Whether we like classic fairy tales or not, whether we think they're blissfully romantic or absurdly outdated, we still respond to them instinctively—almost as if we were born knowing them. Whether you grew up with the *Arabian Nights* or Sanskrit epics or were raised with Hans Christian Andersen, Charles Perrault, and the Brothers Grimm—fairy tales are an unshakeable part of our culture and play an irrevocable role in our psyches.

Yet some critics insist we must try to resist their allure; they claim fairy tales do nothing but fill children's heads with unrealistic, aspirational nonsense. (And I can personally attest to this point of view; the phrase "life isn't a fairy tale" has been hurled at me more times than I can count.) I respond to this by saying it is only by believing the impossible that we can ever learn to reach beyond ourselves and achieve the possible.

But there is more to fairytale wisdom than that. On the surface, fairy tales attack preconceived ideas and warn us not to judge others too quickly: monsters turn out to be princes; peasants become princesses; old crones emerge as benevolent fairies. Even in *Frozen* the villain is a dreamy-looking prince who sings a catchy love song.

Still, some parents worry that even with Disney's sanitized retelling, ancient fairytale themes are simply not appropriate for today's preschoolers. And I can see where they're coming from: all those dead parents, homicidal huntsmen, and evil curses—not to mention all the hard labor. But those dark and disturbing plot strands are precisely the point. Stories that involve oppressive families or desperate poverty help children confront the lesser hardships found in their everyday reality. And all those orphaned princesses and absent mothers speak to their genuine fear of loss.

And although this latter theme may seem a bit macabre, it didn't come out of nowhere. Historically, death through childbirth was the most frequent cause of female fatality, so absent mothers were not at all uncommon (hence all those single fathers you find in tales like *The Little Mermaid*, *Beauty and the Beast*, and *Aladdin)*, and surviving orphans were frequently raised by a mother's successor (hence the stepmothers in *Snow White* and *Cinderella*).

"Even when they seem to be about distant realms that never existed," observes Jack Zipes, author of *Why Fairy Tales Stick*, "every fairy tale is a metaphorical reflection about real conditions in our own societies."[7]

That's the thing—fairy tales are not just about kingdoms far away; they are about the here and now. They are about the injustice, intolerance, jealousy, tyranny, and poverty that are still happening today, in our own backyards.

But is this why they connect with us so deeply? Is this why we respond to them on such a gut level? Why is it that these very simple stories have such an indistinguishable power to enchant us?

"Fairy tales are coded wisdom about how to grow up," explains mythologist Marina Warner.[8]

In *The Uses of Enchantment*, (the first book of its time attempting to explain the hidden meanings of fairy tales using psychology), author Bruno Bettelheim further explains that these ancient narratives show children how life's struggles are "an intrinsic part of human existence."[9] Fairy tales assure us that although unjust hardships are inevitable, with a bit of kindness, compassion, and bravery, you can and will "emerge victorious."

(During my childhood, this translated to the following: yes, life with the hippies will be difficult, even humiliating. But if you work hard and stay focused, one day you will escape and be seen for who you truly are.)

THE PROGRESSIVE PRINCESSES

. . .

THE LITTLE MERMAID (1989) was released just as I became a teenager, and therefore it had a rather profound effect on me. Ariel, the film's aquatic heroine, is feisty and intelligent—and works to achieve a goal that she has set for herself rather than simply responding to a hardship that has befallen her. Long before Ariel sets eyes on Prince Eric, she dreams of living in a world where she is not only accepted but valued. She holds tight to this dream even as those around her insist that she should embrace the underwater world into which she was born.

Ariel is hardly a passive damsel in distress. Yet countless critics have ruthlessly condemned this visionary young mermaid because, and I quote, she "gave up her voice for a man."

When I first came across this interpretation, I was stunned. I was also insulted. Because, to me, Ariel was the strongest, most inspiring princess of all.

When I was fourteen, I had a summer babysitting job for a darling three-year-old girl named Tara. Every day, she and I would settle down to watch *The Little Mermaid* video before her morning nap. Tara usually fell asleep after fifteen minutes, but I would continue to sit on the sofa and watch the movie in its entirety (quite conveniently, the movie usually ended right about the time Tara woke up). I probably watched it close to fifty times that summer. I never got tired of it.

I was not Disney's target market by a long shot, but that movie pierced the very depths of my teenage soul. Ariel wanted to escape her underwater world and live on land; I wanted to escape my rural hippie home and live in London. Like me, Ariel was smart, and she was loved—but that didn't stop either of us from wanting something beyond the life we'd been born into. Ariel's mer-family told her she was crazy to want to live among bipedal humans; my family told me I was crazy to want to live in classist Britain. But neither of us listened to our families. Instead, Ariel and I listened to our hearts. Yes, we made sacrifices (she temporarily gave up her voice, I permanently took on a colossal student debt)—but we did these things not for men but so we could enter a world where we felt *we belonged.*

To me, that is strength. To me, that is bravery. To me, that is being true to the very core of yourself.

When Ariel saved Prince Eric from drowning (another thing critics rarely give her credit for), she saw a glimpse of what human life could be like. She suddenly saw how close she was to her dream, and she went after it with everything she had. So when she pushed herself up onto that rock and belted out a few bars about her destiny while the waves crashed behind her—I cried real tears. Every single time. Because, again, I knew I was no longer alone in the world. Again, I had found someone who truly understood the achings of my heart.

Yes, this little mermaid risked everything for the *possibility* of true love. And people continue to present me with this accusation as if it's a bad thing. But my reply is this: Why *shouldn't* she risk everything for the possibility of true love? In the wise words of renowned feminist Erica Jong, "Love is everything it's cracked up to be. It really is worth fighting for, being brave for, risking everything for. And the trouble is, if you don't risk everything, you risk even more."[10] More than any of the Disney princesses, Ariel understood this.

Yes, true love can lead to vulnerability, and unfortunately our culture views vulnerability as a weakness. But as feminist blogger Justine Musk points out, "Vulnerability is actually a high-risk endeavor."[11] And do we view male risk-takers as weak? No—we applaud them.

So perhaps we should stop dismissing Ariel—and start applauding her.

THERE IS A POPULAR parenting blog called *Princess-Free Zone* that declares:

> The more options girls have, the better. Ultimately, they need to develop not only the princess qualities of kindness, friendliness and modesty, but also the critically important traits of self-determination, confidence, adventurousness, and healthy risk-taking.[12]

Um, who says the latter qualities aren't princessy? Have they watched any Disney princess movies since the 1950s?

Because *Snow White* and *Cinderella* are Disney's most successful princess films, the idea that all Disney princesses (including the modern ones) are "weak and passive" has gained almost unquestioned acceptance. But, other than sweet-natured kindness, modern Disney princesses, (who arrived on the scene more than fifty years later), actually have very little in common with their "angel-in-the-house" predecessors.

The second-wave princesses are headstrong and independent. They engineer their own fates and believe that respect is a precursor to love. And if there is one thing any of the modern princesses are not doing, it's sitting around waiting to be rescued. In the words of Meg Cabot, author of the best-selling *Princess Diaries*, "Princesses have been rescuing themselves for quite some time now."[13]

In Disney's *Aladdin* (1992), Princess Jasmine wants her future husband to marry her for love, not for status. ("I am not a prize to be won!" she shouts.) From the very beginning, she makes it clear to us that being a princess does not guarantee happiness and shows that she is actually willing to give up her royal title if it means she can maintain some level of personal freedom. We watch Jasmine fight hard against the idea of any arranged royal marriage, and her persistence ultimately prompts the abolishment of forced betrothal in her kingdom. At the end of the movie, Jasmine actively chooses Aladdin as her husband—not because of his power or wealth but because he appeals to her intelligence, curiosity, and sense of the adventure.

Although *The Princess and the Frog* (2009) is drastically altered from the original *Frog Prince* fairy tale as told by the Brothers Grimm, the Disney heroine is still a strong one. Whether in frog or human form, Tiana speaks her mind, knows what she wants, and works hard to get there despite criticism from her boss, her friends, and even her family. While Tiana's mother wants grandchildren, Tiana's only focus is to open her own restaurant. The movie contains healthy themes of entrepreneurship and division of labor in the household, and while Tiana is happy to live out her life as a frog as long as she can be with the man that she loves, it is her transformation into a princess that ultimately breaks the amphibian spell. (The name Tiana is a derivative of *tia*, which means "princess" in Greek.)

I've always believed that it takes more than a crown to be a princess; that it's actually how you conduct yourself that truly makes you royal. And fully proving my point, both Pocahontas and Mulan are included within the official Princess Collection, even though neither girl is born royal or marries a prince.

Pocahontas (1995) was the first Disney movie based on a historical event rather than a fictional fairy tale, but the inclusion of Pocahontas within the princess canon is still fraught with controversy. Because while Pocahontas is indeed the beloved daughter of a Powhatan chief, this does not make her a princess in the European sense—the title of chief is an elected one, not a role that one inherits.

Nevertheless, in the movie, the character of Pocahontas is delightfully curious, open minded, and spiritual with a wisdom beyond her years. Pocahontas has no interest in marrying the best warrior because she would rather go cliff diving by herself. Her song "Colors of the Wind" beautifully describes the connectivity of all nature and is a glorious call to action when it comes to protecting the environment. Seeking to prevent further violent conflict between her tribe and the English settlers, Pocahontas dramatically shields John Smith from her father's war club—making a strong statement about the power of tolerance and understanding versus actions taken in blind rage. And in the end, Pocahontas turns her back on romance in order to stay with her people.

Not surprisingly, the movie takes much liberty with historical facts (it also contains talking trees), but what is widely acknowledged to be historically accurate is that John Smith's life *was* saved by a girl named Pocahontas. No tiara in sight, but this single noble act couldn't be more regal.

Based on a legend from medieval China, *Mulan* (1998) is the story of a girl who is fed up with her family's traditional expectations for young women, so she disguises herself as a man and covertly joins the Imperial Army. Mulan ultimately becomes a war hero and earns a prestigious job offer from the emperor himself—proving that her gender has nothing to do with her ability to be a skillful soldier. But Mulan's true strength does not come from her physical feats on the battlefield but from her ability to think strategically and outsmart the enemy. I don't like the underlying theme that in order to be respected you must act like a man in a man's world, but I will overlook that for the time being. What I *do* like is that when Shang falls in love with Mulan it is with her mind, not with her beauty.

Looking at the aforementioned group of animated women, we have to concede that Disney has done pretty well when it comes to diversifying its princess collection. With very little fanfare, they have turned an Arabian princess, an African American waitress, the daughter of a Native American chief, and a Chinese soldier into four of the most familiar female faces in modern pop culture. Can you think of another entertainment genre that has come even close to this?

FIRST PUBLISHED IN 1756 by French novelist Jeanne-Marie Leprince de Beaumont, the story of *Beauty and the Beast* is a moving reflection on the nature of marginalization, of sin and redemption, and the importance of authentic love.

None of this is lost in the animated version.

In Disney's *Beauty and the Beast* (1991), we watch Belle, the film's brainy heroine, flatly reject the sexist and egotistical Gaston, who is widely considered to be the best catch in town. (Belle's natural beauty actually annoys her; she would much rather be left alone with her books.)

Without a hint of resentment, we see her look after her aging father with unbounded patience and love. She fearlessly enters the enchanted castle on his behalf and persists in teaching the Beast to be civilized and kind. Belle eventually falls in love with the Beast not because he is handsome or rich but because—beyond the fur and horns—she sees the beauty of his soul.

"We come to love not by finding a perfect person but by learning to see an imperfect person [or beast] perfectly," says philosopher Sam Keen.[14]

Indeed. Those jaded critics who like to talk about ridiculous things like Stockholm syndrome are absolutely crazy.

But the thing in this movie that really makes me swoon? That *library*. When the Beast shows Belle those towering walls of floor-to-ceiling books, my heart flutters just as much as hers. And although the people in Belle's hometown mock her constant thirst for knowledge, I love that through it all she remains an unabashed bookworm. (And considering I personally hail from a very similar provincial town—one that actually required students to take more PE than math and science—I also sympathize.)

Early on in *Beauty and the Beast*, Belle sings the following:

> *I want adventure in the great wide somewhere;*
> *I want it more than I can stand.*

And for once it might be grand,
to have someone understand,
I want so much more than they've got planned. . .

From the moment I first heard those lyrics nearly twenty years ago, they've had a profound effect on me. Whenever a teacher encouraged me to attend a community college rather than an esteemed East Coast university, I would hum those lines to myself. Whenever I was told that my dreams of moving abroad were unrealistic, I would hum those lines to myself. Whenever my small town made fun of me and my big-city dreams, I would hum those lines to myself. Whenever I chose to sit home and read, rather than succumb to the advances of a dull yet handsome jock, I would hum those lines to myself. Snow White may have got me through kindergarten, but, let me tell you, Belle got me through the perils of high school. And I am overwhelmingly grateful.

HOLLYWOOD ACTRESS EMMA WATSON, a UN Women goodwill ambassador, recently made what many deemed to be a "game-changing" speech about feminism. Launching the HeForShe campaign at the UN Headquarters, Watson explained how gender equality is not a women's issue but a human rights issue, and she received worldwide acclaim for her stance.

Earlier that same year, Watson accepted the role of Belle in the Disney live-action remake of *Beauty and the Beast* (2017). Upon hearing she had been cast as a Disney princess, Watson exclaimed, "My six-year-old self is on the ceiling—heart bursting!"[15]

Clearly, Watson did not see a conflict of interest—because there isn't one. She knows that you can be a princess *and* a feminist, and that they are inherently one and the same.

LETTING IT GO

• • •

AS I WRITE THIS, my daughter is wearing a sparkly blue Elsa dress, twirling around my office and singing "Let It Go" at the top of her lungs. As of last week, I spread icing on a dozen unnaturally blue *Frozen*-themed cupcakes for her third birthday party. And, as of this year, I have been coerced into watching *Frozen* more times than I thought humanly possible (and this is *me* we're talking about; even women who adore princesses have their limits).

Disney's *Frozen* (2013) is the highest-grossing animated film of all time. In less than a year after its release, Disney had sold enough *Frozen* dresses for every four-year-old girl in North America to be wearing one.

But I don't mind all this, because at its heart *Frozen* is about the powerful relationship between two females—a theme rarely found in any entertainment these days, for children or adults.

The movie's Elsa and Anna characters only loosely resemble those from Hans Christian Andersen's 1884 fairy tale *The Snow Queen*—but they still make my princess point absolutely clear.[16] For both Elsa and Anna, being a princess is *not* about finding men to marry but about learning the tremendous power of love versus fear and how love doesn't have to be romantic in order to be magical.

As the film's creators said themselves, "Elsa and Anna are true princesses because they carry the weight of a kingdom on their shoulders, not as the solution to a happy ending."[17]

Whether we live in Arendelle or in Arizona, all women bear the weight of their personal kingdoms. That's why, when it comes to attacking princesses, we really need to "let it go."

TRANSFORMATION

. . .

How could we forget those ancient myths that stand at the beginning of all races, the myths about dragons that at the last moment are transformed into princesses? Perhaps all the dragons in our lives are princesses who are only waiting to see us act, just once, with beauty and courage.

– RAINER MARIA RILKE

MANY ACCUSE THE PRINCESS genre of encouraging young girls (and grown women) to indulge in fantasies of romance and rescue, rather than taking charge of their own lives.

In her fascinating book *Spinning Straw into Gold*, Joan Gould observes that "the more patriarchal the society, the more the heroine is expected to rely on the hero to save her."[18]

Yet this patriarchal slant is not how fairy tales began. Originally, fairy tales were not only about true love but about the *shift in female consciousness* that makes true love possible.

Even in the Disney versions, if we look past the layers of candy-coated romance, we can see that princesses always experience a profound transformation. In most princess narratives, continues Gould, "the aim of the heroine is to arrive before the end at what she was meant to be from the beginning."

Isn't that the ideal aim of our real-life narratives as well?

It's no coincidence that everything we love watching on television involves some sort of fairytale transformation: an ordinary person becomes a celebrity, a cleaning lady becomes a pop star, an ugly duckling becomes a supermodel.

Fairy tales show us that although transformation is inevitable, it's not always easy. Princesses are often forced, by themselves or by others, into the unknown. Think of Beauty bravely entering the castle of the Beast, Rapunzel venturing outside her tower, or the Little Mermaid attempting to navigate a world on legs. Cinderella, Snow White, and Sleeping Beauty all endure strange and often harsh living conditions without the protection of their parents. In the process, all undergo some form of suffering or struggle—yet without this stage of the story, no real change in consciousness is possible. Fairytale heroines must lose their old lives—or be forced out of them—if they are to come into the true life that is waiting for them.

Consider Cinderella. Her transformation takes place the very moment when, along with her rags, she sheds her perception of herself as a lowly, unworthy ash girl. *This* is the moment of change. Not when a man kneels to fit the slipper onto her foot but "when she recognizes that she has turned into the princess she was always meant to be."[19]

(And Cinderella's exquisite crystal shoes have never been just a silly fairytale accessory. Crystals have always been ancient symbols of transcendence—and, when they are placed upon her feet, we see her journey of internal transformation begin.)

"In the whole mythological tradition the woman is already *there*," says renowned philosopher and mythologist Joseph Campbell. "All she has to do is realize it, realize that *she's* the place everyone is trying to get to."[20]

Even Peggy Orenstein admits this. "The biggest surprise of *Aschenputtel*," says Orenstein, "is that it's not about landing a prince. It is about the girl herself: her strength, her perseverance, her cleverness. It is a story, really, about her evolution from child to woman."[21]

Disney's recent and much-lauded *Frozen* lacks the archetypal precision of the original fairy tale, but the timeless theme of transformation remains. Elsa, one of two royal protagonists, has magical ice powers that she can't always control, and, for most of her life, she has isolated herself to avoid harming others. But unable to hide her true self any longer, Elsa escapes her restricted palace life, runs into the Nordic mountains, and euphorically releases the natural-born power she has always repressed. Through this she undergoes a magical makeover: joyously using her unique abilities, she builds the ice palace of her dreams and fiercely independent of any male gaze, her dull palace wear transforms into glittering ice couture.

Likewise, Sleeping Beauty and Snow White did not awake simply because a prince showed up beside them; they awoke because, as women, they were finally ready to consciously step into the glorious lives that always awaited them but they'd previously been blind to. When the Beast lies unconscious waiting to be roused, it is Belle's personal epiphany that saves him. Meanwhile, the gradual metamorphosis in the Little Mermaid is just as much internal as it is physical.

This is a hugely important princess point to drive home: what we often brush off as silly fairytale magic is actually the innate ability women possess to bring about what is already latent within them, to recognize what was always there even though we couldn't see it or because the people around us didn't want us to see it. In fairy tales, it's not enough for princesses to know what they want; they also have to believe that they are entitled to receive it.

The same applies to you. And the same applies to me. The same applies to women everywhere. Deep down, women *know* this. That's why fairytale stories resonate so deeply within our psyches. If only we had the courage to pull the lessons off the page (or the screen) and into our real lives.

But what of the fairytale hero? What about old-fashioned heroics? If fairy tales are truly about female transformation, then where does that leave the handsome prince?

Perhaps "the prince," like everything else in these ancient tales, is merely symbolic.

"When you fight your way through a painful experience," explains author Justine Musk, "when you eat the poisoned apple, . . . or wander through some bleak internal landscape . . . the prize isn't a man on a white horse with a feathered hat, . . . but a more integrated sense of self, a vision for your future that makes you come alive. . . . You wake to look upon your prince's face, and discover that it *is your own*."[22]

So much for misogynistic stories of helplessness and rescue.

As feminist author Naomi Wolf observes, "Isn't it interesting that when fables are filled with actual narratives of female power, assertion and heroism, they are still read as being about beauty and passivity?"[23]

It's more than interesting. If women truly want to live happily ever after, it's something we must strive to change.

Chapter II

IN DEFENSE OF PRINCESS PLAY

· · · · ·

*Can you remember who you were before the
world told you who you should be?*

— DANIELLE LAPORTE

I N MY FAMILY, I was the only granddaughter. So throughout
my childhood, my constant playmates were my little brother
and my two male cousins—each of us about a year apart in
age. Rather than submit to the boys' constant games of combat
or gross mad scientist labs, I often suggested (or, to be fair, often
insisted) that we play "royal family."

I dressed all the boys in a mishmash of items from my extensive
"royal wardrobe" (all of which my mother had purchased from the
Salvation Army), and, with a little female cunning, I was able to get
the boys into the swing of it without relinquishing complete control
of the game. In my imaginary kingdom, I was bestowed with the
title of Princess Royal, my older cousin was not the king (merely
my prince consort), and my little brother was granted the esteemed
honor of acting as our royal guard (he liked this role because he got

to wear his Superman cape and carry an extra plastic sword). And because one can never have too many princesses, we dressed my poor little cousin Christopher in a lacy blue evening dress and told him that although we were letting him be the younger princess, sadly his place in the succession meant he would never inherit the title of queen.

I speak from experience; princess play is anything but passive. For me, it was totally empowering. I sat in the throne. Not the boys.

SOVEREIGNTY

. . .

Your crown is your best friend forever, by far.
It tells the true story of just who you are.

— FROM THE CHILDREN'S BOOK *THE CROWN ON YOUR HEAD*,
BY NANCY TILLMAN

IN THE COURTLY LEGEND of *Sir Gawain and Lady Ragnell* (A *Beauty and the Beast* story where the gender roles are reversed), King Arthur's kingdom of Camelot, as well as his life, will be spared by the evil Black Knight if the King can correctly answer a single question: "What is it that women most desire?"

After a harrowing seven-day quest, King Arthur discovers that the answer is simple: *sovereignty.*

It was true in the sixth century. And it's true now.

Sovereignty can be defined as royal rank, authority, or power; complete independence or rightful status. In essence, it is a woman's royal right to exercise her will. Sovereignty is our true nature, what calls most deeply. And although sovereignty exists in all living beings, it is most evident in our children.

In some cultures, honoring the true nature of others is reflected in the custom of bowing. Instead of shaking hands, you put your palms together over your heart and bend toward each other. Symbolically, this means "the divine in me honors the divine in you" (or *namaste* for those that do yoga), signifying a shared recognition of what is deepest and most fundamental in all of us.

But interestingly, in the West, we only use the bow when greeting royalty. A polite bow or curtsey recognizes the sovereignty of a monarch—and without this collective recognition on behalf of the people, royal institutions literally cannot survive. This same recognition is key to the concept of princess play: girls want the world to recognize their unique sovereignty and to honor the divine within them.

Author Marianne Williamson says that too often we adults ask ourselves, "Who am I to be brilliant, gorgeous, talented, fabulous?" When actually, she says, "Who are you *not* to be? . . . We are all meant to shine, as children do."[1]

Unconsciously or not, that's what our tiara-headed, tutu-wearing, wand-wielding, *Frozen*-singing girls are doing. They are letting their souls shine. And who are we to stop them?

Royal symbolism is fascinating, and even more fascinating is how children are intuitively drawn to it, even though the concepts are thousands of years old. For example, you'll notice that, during royal enactment, children often use scepters and wands interchangeably.

A royal scepter symbolizes both the monarch's temporal power and her spiritual role, while wands represent the power we all possess to turn our intentions into reality (*abracadabra* is actually an Aramaic phrase meaning "I create as I speak"). But, throughout antiquity, staffs of some kind have always symbolized *sovereignty*.

The idea of inherent sovereignty in children can easily be misconstrued to suggest that kids should be waited on hand and foot or allowed to misbehave without limits. But true sovereignty is different from unbridled entitlement. Honoring true sovereignty within our children simply means letting them express their greatness without judgment. Even if it means letting them dress up as princesses.

"When my 4-year-old daughter told me the other day that she was 'ready for princesses,' part of me died," bemoaned computer programmer David Auerbach in *Slate* magazine.[2]

But why?

Book critic Liz Burns calls this phenomena "princess shaming"— which is a great term for it. It's annoying, Burns explains, because "princess culture gives a girl a world where, as a female, she can take center stage. She is the main character; with the men providing supporting roles. There is no need for the child playing princess to imagine herself as the hero: *the princess is already the hero*."[3]

Meg Cabot's hugely popular book series The Princess Diaries (based on the fictional premise that a normal teenage girl finds herself heir to a European throne) has been published in thirty-eight countries, sold more than 5 million copies in the US alone, and been made into two feature films starring Anne Hathaway and Julie Andrews.

When I asked Cabot why she thinks this royal theme hit such a chord with young girls across the world, she explained, "There are those who will always argue that the popularity of princesses is due to the potential gain of material riches, but I think there's something much deeper going on: Girls are often made to believe they are the weakest members of our society. Yet princesses represent a world of female independence, choice and empowerment that isn't found anywhere else."

This is why, when little girls announce that they "are ready for princesses," parents ought to rejoice. Our daughters intrinsically understand that a princess is a woman with true sovereignty, and as adults we must be careful not to actively dispute this by calling for all princess paraphernalia to be thrown onto a bonfire.

It's okay to become frustrated with the excessiveness of princess-themed marketing, but we mustn't scorn it. Dr. Amy Tuteur of Harvard Medical School believes that, by rejecting all princesses, we are inadvertently "teaching girls to distrust their own desires, suppress their wishes, and worst of all, that femininity is a source of shame."[4]

But by *allowing* princess play? We can teach the opposite:

That girls' feelings matter.

That their dreams have value.

That being born female is a blessing, not a curse.

SNOW WHITE WOULD NEVER DO THAT

. . .

EARLIER THIS YEAR, I sat in a London playground and watched a three- or four-year-old girl join a group of little boys who were kicking around a soccer ball. Right away, the girl's father intervened.

"Girls don't play ball," I heard him tell her. "Why don't you go inside that playhouse and make sure that it's tidy?" He wasn't joking.

I was so shocked that I couldn't bring myself to speak. And, to this day, I feel awful that I didn't confront this stranger about his undoubtedly damaging and sexist parenting style.

That said, pushing girls to do something they don't want to do or something that is merely expected of them because they are girls is categorically not something I condone.

But, just as my parents never ordered me to tidy up my playhouse instead of playing ball, they never pushed me into my princess phase or banned me from having one. To me, dressing up as a princess was always something I *wanted* to do, not something my family, my peers, or any facet of society told me I *had* to do. And although I completely understand that some would prefer their daughters dream of soccer balls rather than royal balls, we need to let girls make their own decisions.

The only way I see that princess play can be harmful is if it involves too much pampering; no one wants to raise a royal pain. But brattiness and entitlement are *not* what princesses are about— and we are shortchanging our daughters if we watch Disney movies, read fairy tales, or engage in princess play without attempting dialogue about the royal merits of kindness, respect, and generosity and the real responsibility that all princesses inherit—which is to improve the lives of everyone in their kingdom. We should be teaching girls that if someone tells them they are acting like a princess, it's a compliment of the highest order.

My own parents used to purposely *evoke* my princess obsession if my behavior ever became disrespectful or too self-absorbed.

"Snow White would never do that," my mom would tell me sternly. It was a stroke of genius. And it worked.

THROUGHOUT PRIMARY SCHOOL, MY favorite book was *A Little Princess*, by Frances Hodgson Burnett. (And, now that I'm an adult, it still easily falls into my top ten books of all time.) In the story, Sara Crewe is a privileged ten-year-old girl who suddenly becomes orphaned and forced to work as a scullery maid in the elite London boarding school she used to attend. When faced with this hardship, of all possibilities, Sara pretends to be a princess. This allows her not only to distract herself from her miserable circumstances but to stay true to the goodness within herself.

"It's easy to be a princess if dressed in a cloth of gold," she tells the young pupils who still adore her, "But isn't it a great deal more of a triumph to be one all the time when no one knows it?"[5]

Think about that for a minute . . . as those words are the secret to princesshood.

Playing princess requires more than a fancy gown and a sparkling tiara. A true princess is about knowing your worth and believing in yourself and your dreams. It's about being noble, kind, and compassionate, and embracing the royal virtues of benevolence and mercy. It's about looking after the well-being of your entire kingdom by standing up for what you believe in, protecting those who can't protect themselves, and using your privilege not just to enrich your own life—but for the greater good of your realm. And while a true princess knows she can risk her heart if she meets someone worthy, ultimately she understands that the only person who can really rescue her—is herself.

If more of the grown women I know felt allowed to embody the true power of the princess archetype during their childhood, much would be different. They might stop dating such losers. They might have the courage to ask for a raise. They might aim for goals that are worthy of them. They might stop worrying so much about the voices of others and start listening to the voice within. They might seek their place in the bigger picture and ask themselves how they might empower others to do the same. Most importantly? They might stop thinking that a mediocre life is enough.

WHAT THEY'RE DOING ANYWAY

. . .

CONCERNED WITH ALL THE princess-related rumors, Dr. Sharon Hayes and Dr. Stacey Tantleff-Dunn set out to discover whether Disney princesses actually had harmful effects on young girls when it came to issues of vanity and body image.[6] So they gathered a group of 121 preschool-aged girls. Half the girls watched clips of animated princess movies that featured young, beautiful heroines, and the rest of the girls watched clips of animated children's movies without princess themes, such as *Dora the Explorer* and *Clifford the Big Red Dog*.

Afterward, all the girls were brought together to play in a room filled with a hodgepodge of toys: dolls, dinosaurs, building blocks, free-standing mirrors, and racks of various costumes, including plenty of princess dresses.

It was expected that the girls who watched princess clips would spend more time than the others in appearance-related play like dress-up, but this was not the case. The observers actually found no statistical difference between the play choice of the girls who watched princess clips and those who did not. Instead of immediately diving for the dresses and preening in the mirror, if anything the "princess girls" replicated princess personalities—their behavior was kinder, more generous, and more helpful. "Who's the fairest of them all" was truly the last thing on their minds.

Feminist author Naomi Wolf alluded to this when she explained that perceptions of beauty "are actually about prescribing behavior, not about appearance."[7]

Many mistakenly assume Wolf is on the antiprincess side of the fence, but she's not. She gets it.

"Don't worry if your 5-year-old girl insists on a pink frilly princess dress," Wolf said recently. "It doesn't mean she wants to subside into froth; it just means, sensibly enough for her, that she wants to take over the world."[8]

Amen.

There's a huge gap between the way girls experience princess play and the way adults choose to interpret their actions. As a result of this misconception, many adults unwittingly perpetuate the negative princess stereotype, rather than the gamut of exceedingly good qualities (leadership, diplomacy, compassion, and so on) that princess play can bring about.

More often than not, the problems that princess detractors are keen to highlight have nothing to do with actual princesses but with our adult tendency to frame everything in a commercial context.

Consider the uproar that kicked off when Disney decided to group their princesses into the Princess Collection. I remember the first time I came across such a product—I was in college and picked up a CD from a music store that contained nothing but Disney princess songs. It was hardly an earth-shattering concept. And at the time, bringing the princesses together in such a way seemed so obvious to me—and I had often wondered why it hadn't been done by Disney years before.

Although Disney is constantly demonized for using this multi-princess technique to increase selling potential, I truly believe the Princess Collection is a force for good. Grouping the royal women together allows girls to focus on the magnificent State of Being a Princess rather than the pre-scripted Disney narratives. Standing together, the unique strengths of the individual princesses are amplified, delivering a powerful message to young girls about the force of female solidarity: royal or not, let's stop judging each other and start supporting each other. Because none of us can succeed in life unless all of us are allowed to.

"Whether these toys have become lucrative moneymakers because girls don't have better options, or because their parents and grandparents cling to old-fashioned ideas about what girls want to play with, seems almost beside the point," says Yael Kohem in *New York* magazine. "The fact is, they're selling—so presumably some girls (maybe many) like the way these products are marketed."[9]

Andy Mooney, chairman of Disney's Consumer Products, is widely credited with conceiving the idea of the Princess Collection after he attended a Disney on Ice show in 2000. It was here that he witnessed thousands of little girls dressed in homemade, unbranded princess outfits. Up until then, Disney had somehow not noticed this widespread princess phenomenon. (Seriously, if only Disney had hired me straight out of high school to be their consultant.)

The very next day Mooney ordered his team to create a collection of products that would "allow girls to do *what they're doing anyway.*"

We must remember this: *the demand existed before the marketing.*

The result? The first Princess Collection products were released with no marketing plan, no focus groups, and no advertising. Sales swiftly soared to $300 million. By 2012, that number had ballooned to $5 billion. That's not just clever cross-product promotion. That's filling a canyon-sized consumer demand.

"I don't think any of us grasped how much girls wanted this," Mooney said of the Princess Collection. "It's clear they believe in the unifying attributes of the Disney princesses."[10]

And you know what? So do I.

Two women are more powerful than one. Four women are more powerful than two. But six, eight, ten *princesses?* That kind of power is infinite. And when little girls get together and play princess concurrently? Let me tell you, they know exactly what they're doing.

ROYAL RESCUE

. . .

AS THE HAZY, SLEEP-DEPRIVED mother of a new baby, I was determined to give my daughter every advantage in life: organic baby food, exposure to classical music, the gift of fluency in multiple languages. (My only languages are American English and British English—and living in Europe I am ridiculed for this—so I felt particularly strongly about the latter.)

I'd read somewhere that babies had a vital "linguistic window" between twelve and eighteen months, so I knew I had to act quickly. But I wanted my daughter's bilingual experience to be something we could share, not something I simply subjected her to without understanding any of it myself.

Finally, I came upon a solution: I purchased several Disney princesses movies in French and Spanish. (*The Little Mermaid* was now *La Sirenita* and *La Petite Sirène; Tangled* was now *Enredados* and *Raiponce*.) The plan was to watch them together. She would hear French and Spanish, and since I already knew the characters, songs, and plotlines verbatim, I could provide commentary in English.

It was a brilliant plan in theory, less so in execution—mainly because I discovered that toddlers aren't especially entranced with anything besides *Sesame Street* for more than five minutes at a time before heading off to something new, preferably three-dimensional. But a few months after her first birthday, everything changed. She found *La Petite Sirène* on the shelf and brought it over to me.

Contrary to popular assumption, up to this point I had not flooded my daughter with Disney branding. Her room was full of crown motifs galore, but it was painted "Elephant's Breath," not pink. I had been given plenty of gorgeous baby dresses for her to wear, but she couldn't play in them, so she mainly wore leggings. She did not own a single Disney-themed book, toy, or piece of clothing (other than a small, stuffed Nemo fish whose big eyes she adored).

So, when she brought *The Little Mermaid* DVD over to me and gestured for me to make it work on the TV, I was doubtful it would have a major effect on her. But I was wrong. Despite the French immersion, she was enthralled.

"More Cincess Fish! More Cincess Fish!" she'd exclaim excitedly. How could I say no to that? So I let her watch it for twenty minutes a day.

As the bilingual viewings continued on those dark and rainy London afternoons, I realized that exactly twenty-five years had passed since the movie's original release. The toddler on the sofa with me was now my own, but nothing else had changed. It was still one of my favorite movies and that "Princess Fish" was still a girl after my own heart.

Although I hated plastic clutter, I finally broke down and bought some Little Mermaid figurines off eBay for her to play with. I decided to keep them with the bath toys, since most of the story takes place in the water.

Needless to say, Ariel, Flounder, Sebastian, and Co. quickly became favorite bath time companions. But, as the months went on and my daughter's ability to role-play increased, I was struck by the scene that she loved to play out again and again.

It began by placing Prince Eric in a yellow plastic duck boat, and, before he had a chance to enjoy the ride, she would force the vessel to capsize. Inevitably, Prince Eric would sink to the bottom of the tub. Luckily, Cincess Fish was on hand to brave the bubbles, swim underwater, and pull Eric back to the safety of the surface. She rescued that poor plastic prince over and over again—so quickly and in such repetition that it was often akin to waterboarding.

But what's interesting is that the princess message her toddler mind took away was not the handsome prince rescuing the poor princess in distress—but the complete opposite.

GIRLS WITH DREAMS BECOME WOMEN WITH VISION

. . .

GIRLS ARE SMARTER THAN we give them credit for.

Just because something may seem limiting to adult eyes doesn't mean children will keep it that way. As I've already explained in the previous chapter, Disney is not a terrible starting point, but if girls see something in a story they dislike or something they want to improve—they will change it.

Indiana University conducted a three-year study of kindergarten-aged girls who regularly played with Disney princess dolls, and their research revealed that the girls "repeatedly rewrote plots they knew by heart and subtly altered character roles to take up even more empowered identity positions." Any "restrictive stereotypical roles" actually prompted the children to "improvise" and "to overcome any gendered obstacles that blocked more satisfying identity performances."[11]

In another study, Professor Sarah Coyne of Brigham Young University was inspired by her three-year-old daughter to conduct further research on how Disney princesses influence young girls.[12] Coyne's study found that the girls who were most indoctrinated into the "princess lifestyle" displayed more gender stereotyping, but they also had higher prosocial behavior (read: they were kinder), lower aggression, and better body image (the latter of which was not predicted to be found in the study).

Dr. Michael Gurian, author of *The Wonder of Girls: Understanding the Hidden Nature of Our Daughters*, says, "I have poured through all the research I can find on what negatively affects girls. Playing with princesses while young has not shown up as a red flag in any scientific inquiry."[13]

Despite this, many continue to claim that princess culture promotes unrealistic, brainless, and materialistic goals for young girls. But I find these sweeping accusations to be incredibly hypocritical.

Why are boys allowed to dream about becoming professional athletes rather than careers that "use their brains"? What about parents who encourage their kids to become doctors and lawyers? Does professional earning power not factor into these desires? And growing up to be a pirate or a wizard isn't particularly realistic, so should children never pretend to be those things?

And I'm not the only thinking woman questioning the contradictions of the antiprincess stance.

Yael Kohem of *New York* magazine said, "A boy dressing up like Iron Man, a narcissistic arms mogul turned superhero, is not seen to be nearly as silly or damaging as a girl wearing an Elsa costume, even though they play to the same fantasy impulses. . . . No one assumes boys who play with Nerf guns really believe they'll grow up to be space-soldiers or cowboys. Why not grant girls the same sort of imaginative freedom?"[14]

Allison Benedikt of *Slate* magazine concurred: "Why is it any likelier that your daughter is going to end up thinking that a prince will save her than it is that my son will think he should kill bad guys? Why is one of those fantasies considered damaging and the other harmless?"[15]

We must ask ourselves why we extend such reverence to any aspect of our society that appeals primarily to boys (athletes, violent action heroes, any career that involves cars or rock music), while we systematically dismiss, vilify, or belittle aspects of our society that appeal primarily to girls (princesses, pop music, fashion, etc.).

What's the *real* sexist problem here? The fact that princesses are marketed to girls? Or the fact that society demeans everything that girls like?

ENTREPRENEURS REBECCA MELSKY AND Eva St. Clair recently founded an alternative girls' clothing line called Princess Awesome, which offers dresses featuring dinosaurs, robots, and airplanes among other unconventional "girl" patterns (all selling out faster than they can make them). The women thought long and hard about what to name their company, but they still get criticized because the name they chose contains the word "princess."

But Rebecca and Eva defend their choice, explaining that adults don't always see the allure of a princess from the child's point of view or comprehend how the idea of a princess can be at all empowering. "But to a child," Eva blogged, "a princess *does* have power."[16]

She went on to explain:

Unlike a child, a princess has control over what she does or does not do. She is the powerful daughter in a royal family . . . and will grow up to be Queen, *the ruler* of her land. As a princess, a child can practice how to act and do and be—freed from the control of her normal, regular parents. Even though no child grows up to be a real princess, every child grows up to be an adult with responsibilities—a ruler of some kind. That is the piece most adults are missing.

If we're honest about it, most adults are so focused on improving their external career, they tend not to work on improving their internal character. Yet children are the opposite. When a little girl plays princess, she isn't thinking about something as mundane and defined as her future job or what we adults would term her future "career." Instead, for those precious moments each day when she dances around in her princess gown and plastic tiara, she is literally a queen in the making—acutely focused on the joy of becoming a magnificent woman.

I'm not saying girls should ignore their passions or their skills or not try to figure out what they're really good at and go do it. I'm definitely not saying girls should define themselves through marriage or strive toward nothing but being beautiful and reserved. We all know real life requires hard work and dedication, and allowing girls to play princess doesn't change any of that.

What princess play *does* teach is this: not for one single second should our daughters accept that they are ordinary.

Don't give girls an excuse not to shine.

Because it's the little girls with dreams who grow up to become women with vision.

TIARAS

. . .

I'm fairly certain that given a cape and a
nice tiara, I could save the world.

– LEIGH STANDLEY

"SO WHAT IS THE deal with plastic tiaras?" asked an exasperated friend of mine (the father of a five-year-old princess). "My daughter literally hasn't taken hers off since Christmas. I'm getting kind of worried."

Now this tiara-wearing girl is part of an exceptional family that lives ten months of every year on a small boat circumnavigating the ocean and the rest of the time living in obscure ports around the world. When I say my friend's daughter has had minimal commercial influence and no exposure to Disney, I mean it literally.

Still, I smiled at his fatherly innocence.

Try to understand, I told him, that, hundreds of years ago, kings and queens were genuinely considered to be *divine*. Hundreds of years ago, aiming to be royal was the same as aiming for enlightenment, wisdom, and true sovereignty.

I received the usual blank stare.

But, again, I persevered.

I explained that today's little girls don't emerge from the womb understanding the British peerage or the difference between a socialist republic and a constitutional monarchy. To preschool minds, tiaras don't represent these adult ideas surrounding class and power.

But girls *do* know that, somewhere deep inside of them, their soul is seeking greatness. And, quite often, this ancient, archetypal desire is manifested as the simple, straightforward need to be a princess. Which translates to constantly dressing up in princess dresses or refusing to take off a plastic tiara.

"Okay, fine . . . ," he said. "I *kind of* get all that stuff. But what I don't understand is what exactly is so 'empowering' about wearing a shiny circle on your head?"

Isn't it obvious? I explained how a crown is merely a physical representation of a halo—the radiant circle of light surrounding the heads of wise or enlightened spiritual leaders and the universal symbol of higher consciousness. A girl wanting to wear a tiara means that, at the very core of her being, she harbors a desire to become as wise and enlightened as possible; she is ready, before anyone else even realizes it . . .

"To rule the world?" he finished for me.

I beamed at my newest pupil.

"Exactly," I said. "Don't you think we should let her?"

We can't tell a girl she can be anything she wants and then turn around and tell her she can't be a princess. We can't tell girls they have all these choices and then tell them they've made the wrong one. But we *can* help girls understand the vast responsibilities that all princesses inherit and help them to become the wise and loving Queens they are destined to be.

THE *NEW YORK TIMES* recently published a serious piece in their fashion section about the rising popularity of tiaras in the workplace.[17] Others laughed, but I wasn't the least bit surprised that grown women were finally catching on to what little girls have always known (and what many of our female ancestors also knew to be true).

Diamond tiaras are a more decorative type of crown, but they are no less powerful or symbolic. Just like princesses, at first glance, diamonds can appear fragile—when actually they are one of the most invincible substances on earth. Since antiquity, diamonds have been thought to bring victory, strength, fortitude, and courage to their wearers. And it's no coincidence that diamonds are composed of pure carbon—the foundational element of all life.

Quoting women with powerful executive positions at eBay and YouTube, among others, the *New York Times* article described how, "for some professional urbanites, the tiara is becoming the new power scrunchie, a sartorial coup de grace."

Like I said, some people laughed.

But don't dismiss this. There is something quite telling here.

"If you look historically at great, powerful women," said Amanda Miller, a thirty-six-year-old corporate communications manager, "They always finished with something [shiny or bejewelled] on their heads. Think Cleopatra."

Yes!

Think Cleopatra! Think Boadicea, Joan of Arc, and Elizabeth I. Think Eleanor of Aquitaine, Catherine the Great, and Isabella of Castille. Think Queen Victoria! These are not weak women. In fact, all were formidable rulers.

Bianca Marie Carpio, founder of Smitten Creative Services, a social media marketing firm, said, "Tiaras are not something you grow out of. They're something you grow into, realizing that you're a powerful person."

You don't have to explain that to me. And you definitely don't have to explain that to little girls.

Mere weeks later, even President Obama was photographed wearing a tiara alongside a Girl Scout troop from Tulsa, Oklahoma. The troop of eight-year-old-girls had entered a White House science fair for young women in STEM (science, technology, engineering, and mathematics) and were exhibiting a flood-proof bridge project made of Legos. Posing with tiaras was *their* idea—none of them seeing anything contradictory about historically empowering head-gear and girls who like engineering. Of course, some conservatives were up in arms that Obama dared to break gender stereotypes, but many applauded him. As did I. He knew that feminine power was all around him that day—why not join in?[18]

LIGHTSABERS, LASSOS, AND THE POWER OF GRAYSKULL

* * *

SOME PARENTS PREFER TO steer their daughters away from fairy-tale princesses and toward the tougher female heroines found in comic books and science fiction. Iconic characters like Wonder Woman and Princess Leia seem stronger than those portrayed by Disney. They seem safer and somehow better options because they're not wearing big dresses or engaging in traditional narratives that ultimately involve a prince. Instead of going to balls, these royal girls are fighting fictional wars, saving imaginary planets, and not afraid to engage in real physical combat.

In many ways, "action princesses" are no different from fairy-tale princesses in that they represent adventure, transformation, and destiny. But, because they may seem less feminine than conventional princesses, action princess are often assumed to be better role models.

Yet we must be careful not to make too many assumptions regarding who is superior, because there is enough space within imaginative play to accommodate everyone.

Fairytale princesses may specialize in inner strength, but by no means does that make them inferior women. Likewise, physical prowess does not make one less of a princess any more than athletic talent makes one less of a girl.

"With great power comes great responsibility" is not just something that applies to Spiderman; it applies to everyone. And whether wielding a lightsaber, lasso, or the Power of Grayskull, what truly makes these women royal is they use their inherent powers for the greater good.

Princess Leia

. . .

*"Luke, you have a power I don't understand
and will never have."*

"You're wrong, Leia. You have that power too."

— *RETURN OF THE JEDI* (1983)

MY HAIR WAS VERY, very long when I was a child (please refer to
the Rapunzel photo on page 22). To avoid getting tangled up during
my gymnastics classes, I asked my mother to wind my hair into two
donut-shaped buns on the sides of my head à la Princess Leia. It was
the most practical royal solution I could think of.

(Before I continue, I must issue a small disclaimer: my capacity
for trivia pertaining to the finer points of the Star Wars Trilogy
pales compared to my encyclopedic knowledge of Disney or the
Windsor family. But throw a princess into any plot structure, and I
pay attention despite myself.)

In *The Empire Strikes Back*, Obi-Wan Kenobi laments to Yoda
that Luke Skywalker is "our last hope." But Yoda wisely replies,
"No. There is another."

By that, he meant Princess Leia.

Princess Leia Organa of Alderaan (played by Carrie Fisher) is
the daughter of Queen Amidala (played by Natalie Portman), who
was elected queen of her planet at the age of fourteen (clearly no

issues with female leaders in *that* solar system).

Sadly, many only remember Princess Leia for her gold bikini—very similar to how many can't think beyond Kate Middleton's transparent dress. (It's a shame so many prefer to objectify royal women rather than focus on their substance and strength.) But let us remember that like Snow White, Leia is an orphaned princess. And like Princess Diana, Leia chose a life of resistance instead of acquiescence.

Rather than quietly mourning the destruction of her planet and the loss of her family, Princess Leia takes it upon herself to lead a rebel movement, works as a spy for the Rebel Alliance, and eventually becomes a member of the Imperial Senate.

Although Leia prefers diplomacy and has had extensive Jedi training, she is certainly not afraid to speak her mind and does not hesitate to use her weapons if necessary. She is courageous, defiant, and determined (not to mention rather witty), and, when she picks up on Luke's cries for help, it's clear she also has burgeoning psychic powers.

Leia unflinchingly stands up to Darth Vader, who intimidates all but her. And when everyone is trapped, Leia takes matters into her own hands, telling the men that "*somebody* has to save our skins."

Huffington Post writer Hayley Krischer says that when watching Star Wars movies with her young son, she makes him repeat the following mantra: "Don't. Mess. With. The. Princess."[19]

I don't blame her.

What makes Leia truly formidable is her gradual ability to understand and utilize "the force."

Whatever galaxy we find ourselves in, tapping into the collective goodness of the universe is something we're all capable of. And Princess Leia shows us that once you embrace the force, its noble power never leaves you.

She-Ra, Princess of Power

. . .

A female He-Man? This is the worst day of my life!

— SKELETOR

MY LITTLE BROTHER GREW up in the dawn of He-Man dolls, and, by the time he was four, his bedroom was filled with endless Masters of the Universe accessories. I was nine at the time. And, as excessively girly and princess-obsessed as I was, I was fascinated by the imaginary land that my brother's weird, muscley dolls inhabited. I loved that they lived in castles (be it Snake Mountain or Castle Grayskull); I loved that all the characters had an intricate life history and a superpower unique to them; I loved that He-Man was really an ordinary human named Prince Adam and that his sister was a princess. While my brother staged huge battles of good versus evil on his bedroom floor, I would read the little booklets that came with each character and academically assess the combined skills of each kingdom. These toys may have been branded purely for boys, but, to me, they were still a version of royal re-enactment—and, for that reason, I loved them. Stereotypes be damned.

Nearly twenty years later, I went on a date with a guy in London, and over champagne and oysters, all we did was discuss Masters of the Universe characters. He was so impressed by my "impromptu He-Man knowledge" that he sent me flowers the next day.

Future first dates aside, the point is that my parents never made a big deal about me playing with "boy toys," and, similarly, they never made a big deal about my princess obsession (although I'm sure they secretly prayed I would move on soon). They never judged me, and therefore I never bothered to stop and judge myself.

Still, imagine my delight when Mattel introduced She-Ra, "the Princess of Power." She-Ra's alter ego is Princess Adora (twin sister to He-man's Prince Adam), and her superpowers were bestowed through a magical sword that channeled the Power of Grayskull as a force of honor and good.

She-Ra's trajectory is unique in that she eventually becomes a strong, independent female superhero in a world of *other* strong, independent female superheroes (nearly twenty-five in total). Along with a flying unicorn, She-Ra leads a gang of female freedom fighters to save her home planet from an evil tyrannical rule, and proves to be a tactically astute and wholly benevolent leader. She-Ra is impressively acrobatic but generally nonviolent. (As per broadcast standards of the period, in the televised cartoon, both He-Man and She-Ra are not allowed to use their swords as offensive weapons, nor are they allowed to punch or kick anyone directly.)

But, more interesting than any of this is that She-Ra is blessed with innate powers that He-Man does not possess. She can communicate telepathically; she can heal the injured with her hands. She-Ra is *just as strong* as He-Man, but the compassion found in her additional "feminine" powers makes her an even greater force to be reckoned with.

This sacred combination of masculine and feminine strengths is what true princess power is all about. We can't all have magical winged unicorns, but we can certainly strive to bring out the Power of Grayskull within ourselves.

Wonder Woman

. . .

Wonder Woman is psychological propaganda for the new type of woman who I believe should rule the world.

— WILLIAM MARSTON, CREATOR OF WONDER WOMAN

IN 1982, MY COUSINS and I caught a pair of small garter snakes that were slithering though the banks of Colorado's Platte River. I'm not sure how, but we eventually convinced our mothers to let us take them home and keep them as pets. I named mine immediately: *Wonder Woman*.

We kept Wonder Woman in a heated aquarium for a few months, and I watched in awe as she swallowed goldfish and grasshoppers whole, stared in fascination as she magically shed her scaly skin and revealed her smooth new self. Eventually we released Wonder Woman back into the wild, back to the same grassy marsh where we found her. But I've never forgotten her. She was a princess like no other.

That's right. Wonder Woman may have graced the cover of *Ms. Magazine* three times, but first and foremost she is a *princess*. And, to me, it was a fact that defined her.

Her mother is Hippolyta, Queen of the matriarchal Amazons. As an infant princess, Wonder Woman was granted the wisdom of Athena, the beauty of Aphrodite, and the speed of Hermes (Sleeping Beauty and her gift-giving fairies spring to mind here).

The royal baby grows up to be Diana Prince, and, very much like my beloved snake, she is able to shed her civilian identity and reveal her true self: Wonder Woman—ready to destroy Nazi enemies, foil Japanese plots, and expose international spy rings.

William Marston, Wonder Woman's creator, noticed that "not even girls want to be girls if their feminine archetypes lack power. . . . The obvious remedy is to create a feminine character with all the strength of Superman."[20]

And that's exactly what he did.

In a 1942 press release announcing the debut of Wonder Woman, Marston wrote, "The only hope for civilization is the greater freedom, development and equality of women in all fields of human activity. [Through the Wonder Woman stories,] I hope to set a standard of strong, free, courageous womanhood; to combat the idea that women are inferior to men."[21]

"Wonder Woman was specifically and deliberately designed to show not just that women could be brave, but that femininity itself was a kind of superpower," said Noah Berlatsky in the *Atlantic.*[22]

Indeed. For Wonder Woman, love isn't something she sits around and waits for. Rather, it is a power she uses to save the world from the forces of violence and hate.

Some continue to objectify Wonder Woman because she has the audacity to wear knee-high boots. But let's stop judging her appearance for a second and take note of the hugely empowering mythology behind her. What I find especially inspiring about Wonder Woman's back story is the so-called "Code of the Amazons," which is this:

We are a nation of women, dedicated to our sisters, to our gods, and to the peace that is humankind's right. Granted life by Gaea, the goddesses, and the souls of women past, we have been gifted with the mission to unite the people of our world with love and compassion. Man has corrupted many of the laws our gods set forth. So, in their wisdom, the goddesses did create a race of female warriors dedicated to the ideals of uniting all people, all sexes, all races, all creeds. No longer will man rule alone, for now woman stands as an equal to temper his aggression with compassion, lend reason to his rages, and overcome hatred with love. We are the Amazons, and we have come to save mankind.[23]

It kind of makes you wish the Amazons were real, doesn't it?

"Looking back now at the Wonder Woman stories from the 1940s," says Gloria Steinem, "I am amazed by the strength of their feminist message."[24]

This is no coincidence. In *The Secret History of Wonder Woman*, we learn that Marston was strongly influenced by early feminists ever since Emmeline Pankhurst (portrayed by Meryl Streep in *Suffragette*) was banned from speaking on his campus at Harvard.[25] Later, Marston's personal muse became Margaret Sanger, an early American birth control activist.

More than seventy years have passed, and Wonder Woman has yet to go out of print. Her cultural allure is so strong that, in addition to the predictable licensed images found on thermoses and lunch boxes, she has starred in an exhibition at the Metropolitan Museum of Art (MET), launched a special line of MAC cosmetics, and motivated renowned fashion designer Diane Von Furstenberg to create an entire Wonder Woman collection.

MET curator Andrew Bolton said, "When designers look to Wonder Woman there are two things they seem to refer to: her as a symbol of American democracy and her powerful role as an Amazon woman."[26]

For Von Furstenberg, her Wonder Woman collection was always about empowerment. "Wonder Woman is the ultimate symbol of female strength, independence and freedom," she said. "The message is that there's a Wonder Woman inside every one of us."[27]

Wonder Woman inside us all?

I think what she really means is inner princess.

Chapter III

IN DEFENSE OF PINK AND GIRLY

. . . . .

*Why is it that boys can be boys, girls can be boys,
or boys can be girls—but girls can't be girls?*

B
ELIEVE IT OR NOT, you can be obsessed with princesses
as a child and still achieve things later in life. Despite my
royal fascination (or perhaps because I understood early
on that royalty was another form of political power), I have had
the pleasure of working for a US congresswoman as well as for a
British Member of Parliament (who was one of few female MPs
at the time).

I have seen politics up close. I understand that PR coups tend to
overshadow real issues. But sometimes it verges on absurdity.

In the 2015 UK general election campaign, the British Labour
Party used a pink campaign bus to tour the country and highlight
women's issues such as equal pay, maternity leave, childcare, and
domestic violence.

And what did the media do? They completely ignored the very
real and very important issues affecting women's lives and focused
instead on the "patronizing message" of the color pink.

The message?

I ask you: Why does no one ever complain about the "message" of blue or yellow or green? Or navy or beige or periwinkle? What is it about pink that causes such loathing, such unease?

(Especially if we consider how dull our lives would be without pink sunsets and pink champagne.)

I know far too many intelligent women who roll their eyes in disgust when the color is even mentioned—because of course, "pink" might as well be another word for "princess." But they are hardly interchangeable concepts. (When it comes to genuine royal connotations, purple is the color associated with most European monarchies, while orange and yellow are favored by monarchs in Asia and Africa.)

The real issue is that in our culture today, pink means "girly." And girly means feminine.

And, for some reason, admitting a penchant for either is about as socially acceptable as believing in unicorns. Some women think letting pink anywhere near them implies that they're against female empowerment, bad feminists or, at best, weak or silly.

Well, *someone* in this debate is definitely being silly.

"Girly" is not the opposite of empowerment. Femininity is not incompatible with ambition. And pink is just a color, not a dirty word.

Some cultures have long understood that pink can be just as strong, classic, and respectable as blue. When fashion editor Diana Vreeland famously declared that "pink is the navy blue of India," she said it with more than a hint of jealousy.

"Pink is a color that makes most skin tones look better," says psychologist Sally Augustin, who advises businesses on how to use color to their advantage. She explains that hospital rooms shouldn't be pink because doctors might believe patients are healthier than they are. Augustin also asserts that pink is extremely calming; "a great color for lawyers who are conducting mediation or a board room where conversations may get heated."[1]

And while pink apparently has "a message" when it comes to British women, it is not seen to be at all emasculating for British men. In fact, research has found that British men who regularly wear pink shirts to the office earn more and are better qualified than those who favor traditional button-down shirts in white or blue. Men who wear pink are also more confident and receive a greater number of compliments from female colleagues.[2]

But if a man wears a pink shirt to the office in America? We know he is all but inviting an onslaught of heckling.

"In the US, we discriminate against pink," said Michelle Slatalla of popular design blog *Remodelista*. "We consign pink to the baby's bedroom and the guest bath, rather than celebrating it for what it is: a strong, pure colour that makes you feel happy."[3]

Karen Haller, a color psychology expert, says, "When a child gets a hug from its mother, if that hug were a colour, it would be pink."[4]

When Princess Charlotte of Cambridge was born, London's iconic Tower Bridge was bathed in bright pink light; so was the water in the Trafalgar Square fountains. That same day, Her Majesty the Queen greeted a crowd dressed head to toe in the happy, cele-bratory color.

All that said, is it really possible to separate pink from little girls? From princesses? From the barrage of "girly" merchandise aimed at our daughters?

"Princess play has been around for ages as one of the great forms of imaginative play that girls love to engage in," says Rebecca

Hains in her book *The Princess Problem*. "But it wasn't always this commercialized."[5]

Agreed. It has not always been this commercialized.

Or this gender specific.

Or this monochromatic.

Ironically, for most of American history, pink never stood for girly sentimentality. More than a hundred years ago, *all babies* wore only *white* dresses (mainly because they didn't have neutral onesies) and were groomed to look like androgynous cherubs until they could walk. But, today, we want to know the sex of a baby the moment we set eyes on it—and retailers have responded accordingly.

Fashion historian Jo Paoletti says pink originally emerged as an appropriate color for *boys* because it was "a close relative of red, seen as a fiery, manly color."[6] And, because of its historical associations with the Virgin Mary, *blue* was usually the recommended color for girls. (Consider young Wendy and Michael in Disney's *Peter Pan*: she wore blue; he wore pink.)

But after World War II, fashion trends slowly reversed and the new idea that "pink was for girls and blue was for boys" prevailed for about twenty-five years. Then my mom's women's liberation movement came along. And, in line with their strict notions of gender equality, suddenly unisex clothing for children was all the rage. (Lucky me.) Everywhere you looked, kids were wearing striped shirts just like Bert and Ernie.

Primary-colored, gender-neutral clothing and toys remained popular until the 1980s when prenatal testing became the norm. Now that a baby's gender could be revealed well before the birth, parents wanted to celebrate with pink or blue nurseries, clothing, and parties. As a result, the notion that pink is for girls has become so endemic in our society that the color itself can seem irreversibly linked to the evils of gender stereotypes.

I get that. And I get that today's children are surrounded by some of the most relentless stereotyping in retail history. But we must admit that societal obstacles that keep women from reaching the top are a great deal more substantive than their color preferences.

Like all mothers, I hope my three-year-old daughter becomes an independent, smart, and empathetic adult. But if that doesn't happen, I'm afraid the blame falls on me and my lack of parental guidance—not the pink bows in her hair, the pink pillows on her bed, or the pink toys in her room.

"I simply don't see how pink property might limit a girl's sense of her own potential," says Polly Vernon in her book *Hot Feminist*.[7]

I don't see it either. Allowing your daughter a pink bedroom doesn't mean she will never become a member of the Supreme Court or win the Nobel Prize for physics. Nor does it mean she's destined to live a life of wifely compliance. Give girls some credit. And give the poor color a break.

The antipink lobby bothers me, as it often implies that if a little girl likes pink toys, then there is no way she can also be intellectual or self-reliant. Or if she likes princesses, then that automatically makes me (her mother) ambivalent to commercial forces. But, ironically, such stereotypical judgments about girls and women can make antipink campaigners seem just as divisive as the sexist marketing techniques they denounce.

I totally agree that girls need and deserve more choices than the blindingly pink "girl" aisles that exist in most places that sell toys. I understand that all-pink-all-the-time tends to proliferate a rather one-dimensional representation of femininity. And I believe that additional choices should not only be available in aisles labeled "for boys"—as that can confuse girls who want to feel good about being girls. But fighting a ceaseless battle against corporate marketing, boycotting pink products, or insisting on gender-neutral child rearing are not the solutions.

Rather than making pink and girly toys obsolete, we need to start changing our attitudes toward them. Because it's not just girls who get the raw deal; boys suffer too—and, in my opinion, they suffer in a far more worrying way.

Consider this: your son needs a hula hoop for a physics project, yet he refuses to use the hot pink sparkly one that is sold with a pink label in the pink aisle (which, after trawling the toy section, is the only one you can find). If that's where it begins, what other things might boys feel compelled to turn away from because of their pink, feminine connotations? Nurturing? Compassion? Empathy? Feelings of any kind?

Reversing the reputation of pink, girly, and feminine to one of power rather than weakness affects us all. It affects the future of our world.

We need to start honoring *all things* feminine, whether they are indulged in by little girls or little boys, by grown women or grown men. And we can start by believing that pink doesn't automatically equal inferior.

Alice Dreger, a professor of clinical medical humanities and bioethics, best known for her work on sexual development, has strong opinions on the matter:

> It makes me crazy that some of my feminist friends try so hard to
> stop their kids from being gender-typical. I have one such friend

who has a fairy-princess daughter, and she keeps trying to keep her daughter butch, as if she owes this to Susan B. Anthony. I asked my friend, "If your son wanted to wear a pretty pink dress, would you let him?" She turned red and said, "Yes." I answered, "Then why isn't it gender-based oppression to deny your daughter a pretty pink dress?"[8]

There are a lot of mixed messages when it comes to things pink and girly. On one hand, we have Peggy Orenstein telling us her view on why princess culture is detrimental. On the other hand, we have popular blogs like *My Princess Boy* where a mother supports her son's right to love pink, princessy things. Many are furious when spa parties are marketed to little girls yet are thrilled when a J. Crew ad features a little boy wearing bright pink toenail polish.

So let me get this right: Boys can be boys, girls can be boys, or boys can be girls—but girls can't be girls? How did we let this happen? It seems that, in our endless quest to resist gender stereotypes, we still ended up with different standards for different sexes.

My daughter loves tutus and tiaras, just as much as she loves rocket ships, dinosaurs, and slugs. I'm not a personal fan of the slugs, but the way I see it, parents shouldn't ever have to defend their children's preferences—whatever they may be. We need to stop labeling girls as "girly" and just let them be girls. It's not about making girls choose between building blocks and princesses—it's about allowing them to understand that it's perfectly acceptable to love both.

A high school friend of mine has navigated this tricky parenting terrain brilliantly. I've seen her amazing five-year-old daughter build a birdhouse with her very own pink toolset while wearing hot pink, sparkly shoes. I've witnessed her daughter race her dirt bike in a plastic tiara (though I suppose it helps that her mom is a professional cyclist). And I've been invited to one of her daughter's formal tea parties yet was politely reminded before entering that "hiking boots" were part of the mandatory dress code (I didn't have any but was allowed to borrow some).

My friend has empowered her daughter to be strong, capable, *and* feminine, and she has never made her feel as if these traits are incompatible with each other.

Because they're not.

IS THERE ONLY ONE WAY TO BE A GIRL?

. . .

ONE AFTERNOON, MY BABY daughter and I sat in the park eating strawberries, watching girls from a local school during their PE class.

The girls (age eight or nine) were obviously required to run two laps around the park, and my heart ached for the skinny girl at the back who lagged behind. Seeing her struggle really hit a chord with me (I was *always* the last one to finish running laps in PE, and I hated everything about it, physically and socially).

Reliving those awful memories made me want to pull the poor girl aside and tell her that whether or not she could run fast had nothing to do with how successful or happy she would be later in life.

She was now lagging more than a lap behind everyone else, and the rest of the class was getting restless. Finally, some girls started walking back toward her, and I was certain they were going to bully her into going faster or make fun of her for how slow she was going. But instead, they smiled at her; linked arms with her and ran the rest of the way *with her*, cheering her name the whole way.

I cried real tears.

The Dalai Lama has said that "the world will be saved by the Western woman." And, in that moment, I believed it. I hadn't seen anything so beautiful in a very long time. In twelve years of PE, I don't think anyone ever bothered to cheer me on—what a difference it would have made if they had.

At my school, being athletic was the only thing that truly mattered. Our principal knew the name of every single member of our varsity football team or girls' basketball team (and often gave them high fives in the hallways), but I'm certain he couldn't tell you who was president of the National Honor Society or in the running to be class valedictorian.

My classmates didn't care what anyone was wearing unless it was a letter jacket or cheerleading uniform (both of which I lacked). And the best chance I had of fitting in were the days we had to wear our school colors to show support for the upcoming "big game."

I spent twelve years navigating a culture that blatantly valued brawn over brains. It's not that I didn't *want* to be a girl who was academically *and* athletically successful—it's that I couldn't be. The reality was that, no matter how much I trained, I was never going to be able to run a mile or kick a ball as fast, or as well, as everyone wanted me to. It was not my natural forte, and I hated that I was marginalized because of it—especially when I had so many other (more cerebral) talents to offer.

Many accuse princess culture of promoting nothing but an ultrafeminine way of being, but, during my formative years, I *longed* for a place that would value me as a girl with a good brain, not just a sexless athlete with good coordination.

My ongoing royal fantasy world—where you could wear elegant dresses, walk among gorgeous architecture, read books, drink tea, talk to animals, and ultimately help increase the well-being of your kingdom—seemed like *heaven* to me. And perhaps this fantasy holds the same allure for lots of girls.

Is there only one way to be a girl? Of course not. I know better than anyone that some girls genuinely prefer running to royalty—and, in other schools, in different towns, they might even feel ostracized because of it.

I acknowledge that not everyone fits into the same gendered or commercialized stereotype—and that's a good thing. But it works both ways. Some girls—like me—really and truly wanted to stop running and start ruling.

Disney's Pixar film *Brave* is praised for its feisty royal heroine Merida and her unconventional love of sports and weapons. Combined with Merida's rejection of marriage, dresses, and etiquette, she is a welcome alternative to the other Disney princesses who seem more conventional in comparison.

Merida is a different kind of princess because she doesn't lean toward traditional femininity, and her story is refreshing because of that. But, just as critics accuse the earlier Disney princess films of marginalizing little girls who refuse to wear skirts and like to play in the mud, the same can be said about *Brave* in that it ignores the little girls who like princesses because of their heightened femininity, not despite it.

Merida received a minor makeover when she was officially added to the Disney Princess Collection, and there was a huge commotion among the antiprincess movement as a result. Merida's hairstyle changed slightly, and suddenly (gasp) she was wearing a dress. Within minutes, the blogosphere became furious and hysterical.

But let's keep things in perspective. Merida hasn't turned into a bimbo just because her hair is bit smoother. And, when a girl decides to wear a dress one day instead of jeans, it doesn't mean that she is no longer athletic, defiant, and curious. Everyone seems to be forgetting the movie's *main message*: just as there is not one way to be a girl, being "brave" doesn't have just one look.

YOU CAN BE A PRINCESS, BUT YOU CAN BUILD YOUR OWN CASTLE TOO

* * *

TARGET RECENTLY ANNOUNCED ITS bold plans to "remove reference to gender" in their toy aisles. Here in London, the famous Harrods department store has also stopped dividing toys into boy/girl sections and now displays them according to theme (space, nature, etc.).

Slowly but surely, things are moving in the right direction.

But it's not happening as fast it should.

And, as it stands, a lot of people shopping for girls in places other than Target or Harrods won't think to venture beyond the pink "girl aisle." And a lot of little girls won't either. So isn't it better to have pink building blocks and pink chemistry sets in the girl aisle than none at all?

When it comes to pink, princessy marketing on toys that encourage STEM, to me it seems more important to expose girls as much as possible to new types of playthings than it is to appease a stubborn, antipink ideology.

Besides, don't pink blocks work according to the same laws of physics as blue ones? Doesn't a pink lab coat work just as well as a white one? The fact remains that using your brain and the color pink are not mutually exclusive. As long as little girls understand that pink globes and pink Scrabble sets are not considered *inferior* to blue ones, then I see no legitimate harm.

GoldieBlox, a company that creates engineering toys specifically aimed at young girls, understands that girls shouldn't be pigeon-holed. In the words of Lindsey Shepard, their VP of Sales, "It's great to be a princess, but you can build your own castle too."[9]

Despite this progressive stance, GoldieBlox has still been criticized for using pastel colors and a cute, fairytale mascot named Goldie in their product packaging.

But why shouldn't a company utilize a famous fairytale allusion? As I've mentioned before, when it comes to fairy tales, we all instinctively respond. (Albert Einstein himself has said, "If you want your children to be intelligent, read them fairy tales.")

And as for the girly Goldie, I *love* that she has a passion for engineering yet remains true to her feminine self.

I find it offensive that so many assume "girliness" is completely incompatible with STEM. I know more than my fair share of female scientists (that's what happens when you live so close to Oxford); and although these ladies wear goggles and lab coats at work, believe me, when Friday night rolls around, they are the first to don high heels and bouncy blow dries. We need to accept that girls and boys (and men and women) are capable of diverse interests. Don't try to fix it; embrace it!

Still, I know plenty of mothers who flatly refuse to allow their daughters anything pink, anything princess-related, or any toy that is vaguely domestic or maternal because they fear future repercussions. But responding to limitation with further limitation is not the way forward. Although it's wonderful (and necessary) to encourage girls to play with STEM-related toys, in the same vein, we must be wary of banning all others. Because refusing to allow toys that may seem inherently or even stereotypically girly can send a dangerous message: that a girl must choose between being smart and successful (as you define it) and feeling good about herself as a girl.

Melanie Nelson, a PhD-holding scientist, was determined, along with her husband, that their daughters would play only with gender-neutral, science-related toys and was adamant about keeping pink, princessy items out of their house at all costs.

"But we decided the battle was doing more harm than the princesses would," she admits. "We saw that we were inadvertently telling our daughters that their interests weren't 'right' or good enough for us, and that 'girl things' such as princesses weren't as good as the 'boy things' we seemed to prefer. . . . And as much as I disliked some of the messages in the princess stories, I disliked the message my fight against them was sending even more."[10]

In the end, Nelson didn't see princesses as the real problem. "The problem," she said, was "stereotyping an interest in princesses as inconsistent with other interests, such as science and math."

Princesses have *never* been the real problem. The real problem is that we are teaching girls to believe that they can only be part of who they are in order to succeed.

As parents, we must stop reacting to our own preconceived notions of gender correctness and realize that our daughters' preferences may not always match our own. But, more than anything, we must remember that if our daughters know they have our deep, genuine acceptance, this will vastly outweigh any of our adult notions regarding gender, marketing, or colors (much less our personal identities as feminists).

I recently e-mailed another friend of mine, asking why she didn't seem worried about her four-year-old's pink princess obsession, and her reply was this: "I have never doubted that my influence easily outweighs the marketing experts at Disney. I know the world my daughter witnesses every day, the one modeled by her parents, is going to have the most influence on her life."

The simplicity of this answer struck me. And I suddenly felt surprised that more self-proclaimed feminist mothers I'd encountered did not exhibit the same level of comfort.

But here's my hunch: this antipink uproar actually stems from a heartfelt desire to shield all our little girls from the harsh realities of the real world, to protect them from crushing disappointments that might exist in their future.

My hunch is that, once upon a time, most of these antipink crusaders had their own fairytale dreams. (Yep. Even them. Because everyone does.) Yet they grew up and quickly realized that not all people are charming, princes rarely show up on white horses, and nothing guarantees happily ever after.

For most of us, life is harder than we ever imagined it would be. We've stopped dreaming about castles and ball gowns because now we're worried about paying the mortgage and finding the right health insurance, about taking too much maternity leave and not getting promoted. We're worried about pollution in our water, chemicals in our food, bullies on the playground, guns in the class-room, porn on the internet, gang rape on campus, and terrorists in the sky.

So, when little girls look up at us and say, "I want to be a prin-cess," our hearts skip a beat. We panic. And instead of buying her a pink dress or pink toy that we know she'll love, we forge ahead and insist she wear something yellow and play with something wooden, and refuse to take her to see the next Disney princess movie.

As if that alone could protect her. As if that alone could stop her from dreaming.

But I suspect what we really want to whisper back at them is this: "I wanted to be a princess too. In fact, I still want to be one. . . ."

That's the thing about fairytale dreams. They're enduring. They don't go away simply by changing the color scheme. You can paint them any color you want or no color at all, but, mark my words: they can, and will, live on.

Chapter IV

IN DEFENSE OF THE PRINCESS ARCHETYPE

· · · · ·

*The princess archetype is not about passivity
and decorativeness: it is about power
and the recognition of the true self.*

– Naomi Wolf

F OR MY EIGHTH-GRADE HONORS history class, we had to
dress up as our favorite character in history (living or
deceased) and give a five-minute spoken presentation as if
we were that person. I chose Princess Diana, who, at that point in
time, was very much living. I wore navy polka-dots, large shoulder
pads, a pillbox hat, and pearls. At my side was a life-sized cardboard cutout of Prince Charles, complete with a double-breasted
suit jacket and royal sash. (Some idiot at my junior high school
promptly poked Charles in the mouth with a pencil, but it didn't
make me love my English prince any less.)

My fellow classmates toured all the elementary schools with
our troop of characters, and day after day I repeated my perfectly
practiced Diana monologue in my best upper-crust English accent.

Afterward, the children in our audiences sent thank you notes to their favorite characters—and while Thomas Jefferson, Bob Marley, and the Wright brothers received most of the letters from the boys, Princess Diana had the honor of receiving 98 percent of the letters from the girls.

"Thank you for coming to our school. I liked you the best because you were a princess." "I want to be a princess someday." "You are my hero because you are a princess."—and so on and so on.

After one week, I had nearly fifty handwritten letters.

THE POWER OF THE PRINCESS ARCHETYPE

• • •

The power of the princess archetype predates Disney's marketing machine and will no doubt outlive it.

– VIRGINIA POSTREL, *THE POWER OF GLAMOUR*

MANY INSIST THAT PRINCESS idolatry is merely the result of corporate brainwashing that has coerced generations of women to unthinkingly adore the idea of a princess. But it seems *incomprehensible* to me that so many grown women could actively gravitate toward such a strong concept of feminine expression unless there was something that resonated within us on a more profound level.

One reason why princess stories and fairy tales have such a lasting presence in our society is because they tap into our natural human need for relatable archetypes. The princess archetype is so deeply rooted that it has survived through millennia and is present in almost every culture across the globe. In the big scheme of things, Disney princesses are a relatively recent manifestation of this phenomenon—merely scratching the surface of the much larger metaphysical issues stirring beneath.

The concept of archetypes is not just psychobabble. Found in psychology, philosophy, mythology, literature, and folklore, archetypes have shaped our relationships with power and ritual for centuries and are said to represent parts of our personalities that are consistently seeking expression.

Psychologist Carl Jung called these archetypes "images of instincts" or "fundamental blueprints of the self" and believed them to be universal, operating in the psyches of all human beings. Archetypes are said to stem not only from our unique individual histories but also from our collective human unconsciousness.

There are several archetypal images that recur regularly in the human psyche, including Child, Hero, Mother, Wiseman, Patriarch, Fool, Rebel, Warrior and, of course, *Princess*.

"The princess is what you make of her," said Virginia Postrel in the *Wall Street Journal*. "She may be wise-cracking or demure, a blue-eyed blonde or a tawny brunette, goth or Gothic, a domestic goddess like Snow White or a warrior like Xena. The princess archetype is powerful because it is adaptable. It changes with time and circumstance, while retaining its emotional core."[1]

Most little girls express their princess archetype freely and happily—*until* they are told by adults that they must grow out of it (or at least suppress it) in order to conform to society's expectations. The grown-up evidence of this is everywhere.

Super-savvy career women will whisper to me how they still shed a tear on the anniversary of Princess Diana's death—somehow ashamed of the intense emotion evoked by a woman they never met.

Ultra-ambitious college girls will publicly cite Hillary Clinton, Sonia Sotomayor, Sheryl Sandberg, or Marissa Mayer as their role models. But when pressed further? They unanimously confide that the woman they truly want to be is Kate Middleton. "Just don't tell anyone I said that," they beg me. "She's not who I'm supposed to look up to."

"I can't wait to see the new Princess Grace movie with Nicole Kidman," a friend of mine recently admitted, her cheeks flushing with embarrassment. "I have to see it. But I already hate myself for wanting to."

Oh, the heartache and confusion that old-school feminism has created! All of these grown-up women trying their best to suppress the mysterious allure of the princess; all of them afraid it will somehow weaken them in the minds of others if they surrender to her power. All of them torn between adoring (or even emulating) an iconic woman or hating her because they think they're supposed to. You know modern feminism has failed us if choosing to hate women can seem like the correct choice.

Despite how much we indulge or deprive ourselves, the ancient lure of the princess archetype shows no signs of abating. We simply can't get enough of her. We can't stop caring about her. We can't stop loving her. We can't stop wanting to be her.

Nor should we.

If we stopped hating ourselves for loving princesses and began openly embracing all that the archetype represents, translating these traits directly into our everyday lives, I suspect most women would be a great deal happier. And so would our world.

In an era where women are increasingly told that we should behave like men to compete in a man's world, the princess archetype allows women to openly embrace their feminine power. Women who embody the princess archetype unapologetically combine the feminine strengths of grace, empathy, and compassion with the royal virtues of benevolence, generosity, diplomacy, and the desire to enhance the well-being of everyone in the realm. Women who embody the princess archetype are magnetic; their sense of possibility, contagious.

Because we live in a world suffering from extreme masculine bias, connecting with the princess archetype is something women instinctively crave for their own survival. Princesses represent a raw magic that all of us are drawn to—because, unconsciously, we are longing to bring it out in ourselves.

ECLIPSING THE MEN:
FIVE ICONIC PRINCESS ARCHETYPES

. . .

*Archetypal patterns remind us of
our own divine potential.*

– CAROLINE MYSS

DIANA, PRINCESS OF WALES, was a woman, a wife, and a mother who possessed the same hopes, dreams, and insecurities that make up any individual. Yet, at barely twenty years old, Diana became the focus of a collective archetypal projection on a scale that few people in this century have managed to invoke.

Many still puzzle over why this is, but the reason for Diana's mass popularity is simple. At some point, every woman dreams of meeting her own version of Prince Charming, becoming her own version of a princess, and living her own version of happily ever after—and, by agreeing to marry Prince Charles, Diana became a conduit for the world to vicariously live out these desires. Diana fulfilled a very real and deep-seated archetypal need in our global psyche that could not (and cannot) be fulfilled by politicians or Hollywood stars.

Diana's extraordinary princess archetype has been compared to that of Grace Kelly, Jackie Kennedy, and Eva Perón (and is now being compared to Kate Middleton).

Diana, Grace, Jackie, Evita. These women are so well known to us that you need only to hear their first names (not their husband's last names), and you know instantly who they are. All were elegant women who possessed a glamour that was unmistakable yet discreet. (The allure of their style was their worldly nonchalance, never their bling.) But more than this, through their extraordinary grace and compassion, all managed to navigate a masculine world with more skill than most men, single-handedly transforming dynasties that were centuries old.

Each of these iconic women dared us to take them at face value. They are often accused of not having "real careers" (as if an office job is a person's only source of worth), but it is precisely because these women didn't have conventional professions that they challenged us to ascribe value and meaning to who they were, rather than where they worked. For these archetypal women, being themselves *was a job*.

But their defining grace was their generosity. These ladies reached a level of such noble self-empowerment that empowering others became their raison d'être.

All five women listed here attained their status through marriage, yet, through their extraordinary public service and unapologetic feminine strength, each went on to become more influential, more inspirational, more iconic, and more beloved than their husbands who were born into positions of authority.

"I am merely the man that accompanied Jackie Kennedy to Paris," JFK once joked.

And how many of you even know the *name* of Grace Kelly's husband? Or Eva Perón's?

Would any of us pay one iota of attention to the dreary likes of Prince Charles and Prince William if they didn't have such incredible wives? (Or, in Prince William's case, an incredible wife *and* an extraordinary mother?)

The princess archetype allows women to eclipse men, propelling them beyond the mundanity of marriage into an exalted position of feminine power that even if (and sometimes when) the man is dropped—none of us care. When it comes to princesses, the prince is not the point. And never has been.

Diana

. . .

None of us who lived through it will forget that dislocating time, when we saw the archetype clear and plain, the collective psyche at work, the gods pulling our strings . . .

— ROYAL AUTHOR AND HISTORIAN HILARY MANTEL,
DESCRIBING THE DAY DIANA DIED

THE IDEA OF A monarchy somehow answers many of our social, emotional, and often spiritual desires. Part of what made Princess Diana so dazzling is that she intuitively understood this.

Lady Diana Spencer was always a great deal more "royal" than the famous family she married into. I'm not just talking about lineage. I'm talking about her entire way of being. Diana radiated magic. Her mere presence had a transformational effect on whomever she came into contact with. She never wore gloves like her in-laws but greeted the masses with bare hands; many would claim she actually possessed something akin to a healing touch.

Editor Tina Brown called Diana a "compassionate crusader who seemed to become more beautiful the more she shared the miseries of others."[2] Historian Hilary Mantel called her a "carrier of myth."[3] But feminist author Naomi Wolf said it all when she called Diana "a glamorous yet underestimated stealth radical."[4]

Diana didn't marry Prince Charles to undermine his family, but she never could have predicted that, in refusing to conform to the archaic expectations of a royal wife, she would become one of the most famous women in the world.

Although Diana has been analyzed for decades, few give her credit for all she actually accomplished. By the time she was twenty-eight years old—the same age Kate Middleton was when she got engaged—Diana was already actively involved in more than one hundred charity organizations. (When praising Kate, many forget how far behind she is when it comes to following in her mother-in-law's charitable footsteps.)

The British royal family has always supported numerous charities, but Diana transformed this tradition into a tremendous personal calling. It is not an exaggeration to say that, single-handedly, Diana made activism glamorous—paving the way for other celebrities such as Bono, George Clooney, Angelina Jolie, and Emma Watson. By mixing the magic of royalty with humanitarian causes and the worldwide reach of the media, Diana personally created a new kind of princess power.

"Diana's overall effect on charity is probably more significant than any other person's in the 20th century," said Stephen Lee, director of the UK Institute of Charity Fundraising Managers.

Diana recognized that the British monarchy had to change if it wanted to maintain a relationship with its subjects and the world.

And ignoring the barriers of protocol, Diana took it upon herself to embody that change, actively waging a war against the stuffy status quo. She fought her way through the various royal trappings that hemmed her in and learned to use her influence (not her affluence) to further her mission.

Monica Ali, author of *Untold Story* (a novel that imagines an alternative future for Diana if she had lived) is full of praise for the rebellious nature of the late princess:

> For a woman who was uneducated and intellectually insecure, who got engaged at a very inexperienced 19, who lived in the goldfish bowl of media attention, who carried the full weight of expectation that she would put up and shut up about everything—from her husband's infidelity to the suffocating royal protocols—speaking out instead of shrivelling up was not just a sign of wilfulness, but of her determination to direct her loss and suffering outwards. It was a mark of her strength of character; and it's no small wonder that millions of people instinctively responded to that.[5]

Indeed. Diana broke new ground by making the monarchy both glamorous and accessible—adjectives never used to describe it in the past. At a time when the UK class system was even more pronounced than it is today, Diana brazenly embraced low-income families. She made no secret of her struggles with eating disorders and people loved her for her honesty. Buckingham Palace wanted her to attend royally "appropriate" events like the opera, but instead Diana favored concerts by openly gay artists like Elton John and George Michael. Most recoiled from AIDS sufferers in the 1980s, but Diana warmly embraced them and made sure that the world saw her do it. And, after her divorce, when British Muslims were still highly marginalized, Diana didn't hesitate to fall in love with one of them. In retrospect, her behavior was not only brave; it was practically subversive.

Kate Middleton is constantly compared to the woman who would have been her mother-in-law, and even wears Diana's sapphire ring on her finger. But if Diana can teach Kate (and us) anything, it's the power of striking out, of taking a stand, of learning to harness one's privilege and status for the greater good. Diana may have started her journey as an obedient bride, but, in the end, she emerged as a feminist icon.

Personally, I refused to believe anyone when they told me the news of her death. It was nearly 1 a.m. in upstate New York; I was deep in the throes of a college frat party and certain that my friends were playing some vast, practical joke on me and my royal obsession. But, as the evening wore on and more and more people sought me out to reveal the heartbreaking news, I realized that the impossible was true.

I locked myself in my dorm room with piles of newspapers and cried for hours as I poured over the tragic headlines. I stared at the television as the knee-deep sea of flowers piled higher and higher in front of Kensington Palace. I stayed up by myself to watch the 4 a.m. funeral, as all those who pledged to stay up with me fell asleep soon after midnight.

To me, Diana was the personification of my soul's deepest desires. She died young (she was just thirty-six), but, until then, she had been the living link between the fairy tale in my heart and the fairy tale I hoped my life could become.

Her death felt as if some merciless higher power had deliberately plucked the biggest inspiration out of my life, leaving me to face the world alone. No one could console me. (The only person who came close was, quite unexpectedly, my dad—who told me he felt exactly the same way when John Lennon died.)

Many like to refer to Diana as a fairytale princess but we must remember she was human—and her humanity showed us that real princesses endure more than their fairytale counterparts: they argue with their princes, their hearts get broken, their cars crash.

Nearly twenty years later, I still meet women who honor Diana's memory by quietly lighting candles on her birthday or wearing black on the day that she died. And I've slowly come to realize that this constant, inexplicable mourning for a princess we never knew is not really about Diana at all, but *about us*. About our lost dreams, our lost power, our lost heroines.

For a brief but incredible moment in time, Diana allowed us to hear our own call to greatness. She showed us that, as women, we don't have to be perfect (we all have our character flaws, our anxieties, our weaknesses)—but if we *embrace the princess inside us*, we can still be powerful, we can still be feminine, we can still create lasting change and bring about lasting good. (And under no circumstance is a prince required to get the job done.)

She is gone now. But her memory still stirs the most cynical of female hearts. Her memory makes us ache inside because it is a constant call to action—and very few of us are answering.

Grace

* * *

The idea of my life as a fairy tale is itself a fairy tale.

— PRINCESS GRACE OF MONACO

PRINCESS DIANA DIED AT the beginning of my junior year of college, three months before I was scheduled to come to England for the first time. I was beyond devastated. After waiting all my life, the study abroad adventure I had longed for had suddenly become bittersweet; having a chance encounter with my heroine was no longer a farfetched dream but a stark impossibility.

So there I was on my very first morning in London, fighting through my jet lag and placing flowers at the gates of Kensington Palace, overcome with grief for a woman I would never meet.

That summer, as my friends and I backpacked through Europe, I made a point to pay my respects to another fallen princess. Under the guise of showing everyone the glamorous yachts of Monte Carlo, I found myself wandering through the strangely magical principality that is Monaco. While the others basked in the sunshine, snapping photos of sports cars and casinos, I placed flowers on the floor of a darkened cathedral, upon the gravestone of another lost princess: Her Serene Highness Princess Grace of Monaco.

A year later, I was invited to a London party themed "dress as your hero." (The Brits love themes.) As an American on foreign shores, my costume was a no-brainer: I would go as Princess Grace.

Admittedly, my wardrobe already contained a few too many cardigans and circle skirts. So I added some pearls, white gloves, and cat-eye sunglasses, coaxed my hair into retro waves (think early Betty Draper from *Mad Men*), and finished the look with a rhinestone tiara. I proudly spoke with my American accent but told everyone at the party that I had renounced my US citizenship so I could be fully devoted to my new Monegasque kingdom. The Brits thought my earnest attention to detail was hilarious and so very American. But Princess Grace meant the world to me; how could I forgive myself if I failed to do her justice?

Before she became a bona fide princess, Grace Kelly was a glamorous Hollywood star, and, by her early twenties, she was already world famous in her own right. She was beautiful—there is no doubt about that (if I could have the face of anyone on this planet, it would be hers). But she was also talented, and in 1955 she won the Best Actress Oscar for her role as an alcoholic's long-suffering wife in *The Country Girl*. Months later, she played the role of Princess Alexandra in *The Swan*, not knowing that her life would soon imitate her art.

At first glance, Grace seemed to have everything. But, despite her accomplished career, she had not yet found true love. The men she encountered in Hollywood found the combination of her acting success, her earning power, and her immaculate beauty to be far too intimidating.

Except for Prince Rainier of Monaco.

In him, Grace had met her match; someone who would not worship her fame and iconic status but who would love her as an equal. (Grace always knew she deserved nothing less than "a prince," she just happened to find one who had a real title.)

In a media event of staggering proportions, Grace Kelly married Prince Rainier III in 1956 and stepped into the role of Her Serene Highness the Princess of Monaco as easily as if it were scripted for her directly from MGM studios. (Her iconic wedding dress would later serve as the inspiration for Kate's.) And when it comes to beautiful commoners marrying into royalty, Diana and Kate were definitely not alone in having every detail of their nuptials covered by the press.

"Grace moved from an artificial stage to a real one," said her former costar, Gary Cooper. And she did it flawlessly.

Despite the constant media attention on her family, Grace was a mother first and foremost, and lovingly raised three (half-American) children. And while her new life as a princess was enhanced by privilege, it was also enriched by duty. Many didn't think Grace could transition from actress to stateswoman, but she surpassed everyone's expectations and became an extraordinary ambassador for her adopted country.

Grace redefined the role of a modern princess by devoting her public life to the plight of those in need. When she became president of Monaco's Red Cross, she brought in the support of her Hollywood friends, and their fundraising reached unprecedented levels. Later, she founded the AMADE (Association Mondiale des Amis de l'Enfance) charity to promote the United Nations' Convention on the Rights of the Child and was one of the first celebrities to advocate breast-feeding though her public support of La Leche League.

Although the world only witnessed the polished poise Grace projected to the public, those close to her insist that she was even more beautiful on the inside.[6] And it is that inner beauty that allows her royal legacy to endure.

"That is what [Grace] Kelly did," said Anthony Lane in the *New Yorker*. "She caused love . . . and women, no less than men, still devote themselves to her case."[7]

Grace Kelly, like Jackie Kennedy, was an American woman whose destiny allowed her to personify the princess archetype and become a global icon. Grace and Jackie actually had much in common: they were both born in 1929; both hailed from Irish Catholic families; both named their daughters Caroline; and both married into huge, glamorous dynasties—yet ultimately redefined them. But it was Grace's royal life, including the shock of its tragic ending, which more closely parallels the archetypal narrative of Princess Diana.

The two princesses had bonded before Diana's royal wedding at a reception in London. Diana was just nineteen years old, newly engaged to Prince Charles, and this outing was her first "public" date with him. Royals are not supposed to wear black (except when in mourning), yet Diana had unknowingly broken this protocol with a cleavage-revealing (scandalous!), off-the-shoulder gown in black taffeta. To her it was grown-up and glamorous, but, to everyone at the high society party, it was a huge fashion faux pas.

In the ladies powder room, Grace, then fifty-two years old, saw the young Diana break down in tears. The story goes that, in a flood of emotion, Diana revealed her insecurities about the royal engagement and her fears regarding the life without privacy that stretched out before her. Princess Grace, who was more than accustomed to life in a fish bowl, took Diana aside and comforted her. "Don't worry, dear," she laughed gently. "You'll see, it'll only get worse."

Eighteen months later, Princess Grace died from injuries sustained in a car crash that would eerily resemble Diana's own fate.

When Grace died, Diana insisted upon attending the funeral in place of Prince Charles. Buckingham Palace protested, but Diana was so adamant that at last the Queen agreed.

"Diana felt a genuine sisterhood with the deceased princess," said Tina Brown in *The Diana Chronicles*. "Grace [if she had survived] would have been an excellent mentor for Diana."[8]

Brown observed that "the funeral of Princess Grace was like a small scale dress rehearsal for Diana's. As many as 26,000 people filed past Grace's casket in the shadows of the Cathedral [while 100 million watched on TV] and the streets were awash in weeping women."

Thousands of women weeping in the street. Only a true princess can make that happen. Only a true princess can make a teenager raised by hippies, from a whole other country and generation, trek to a tiny European principality and weep silently at the burial site of a woman she never knew.

Such is the power of the princess archetype. We mourn deeply when they are lost. Because it is an aching reminder of the lost princess within ourselves.

Jackie

. . .

I am a woman above all else.

— JACQUELINE KENNEDY

JACKIE ONCE SAID THAT President Kennedy was especially fond of this song lyric:

Don't ever let it be forgot,
that once there was a spot,
for one brief shining moment, that was known
as Camelot.

And we haven't forgotten. Even if we weren't alive to experience the Kennedy mystique, this particular fairy tale still lives on in our hearts—without the help of Disney or a happy ending.

The analogy so often used to describe the Kennedy administration is based on the hit Broadway musical *Camelot*, which depicts King Arthur's realm as nothing less than idyllic. "It alluded to a magic moment in American history," says Theodore White of *Life* magazine. "Gallant men danced with beautiful women, great deeds were done, artists, writers and poets met at the White House and the barbarians beyond the walls were held back."[9]

So while Grace and Diana became real princesses, it was during this era of Camelot that Jackie Kennedy became America's first Queen.

Like all these archetypal women, Jackie was always more than just a pretty face. Shrewdly intelligent, she went to Vassar College, won a writing contest for *Vogue* magazine, and, at only twenty-four years old, was hired by the *Washington Times-Herald* as the "Inquiring Camera Girl" to travel to London and cover Queen Elizabeth II's coronation. Little did Jackie know that, exactly eight years later, she would be married to the US president and dining at Buckingham Palace as the Queen's honored guest. (Oh, to be a fly on the wall at *that* dinner party!)

The Kennedys brought a unique style and charisma to the White House that Washington had never seen before. Jackie and her husband radiated modernity, stability, and family unity, and, for the first time, the presidential couple seemed interesting, even appealing, to those outside of political circles.

"Holding court" is inherent to the royal archetype, and it is something Jackie did extraordinarily well. With Jackie at the helm, White House guests were no longer just boring heads of state; soon they included Nobel laureates, artists, musicians, and intellectuals. Jackie spoke fluent Spanish when visiting Harlem and fluent French when seated next to President de Gaulle.

"Jackie cast a particular spell over the White House that has never been equaled," said Benjamin Bradlee, former editor of the *Washington Post*. "She had great taste, a sense of culture, and a deep understanding of art."[10]

The name Jackie quickly became synonymous with high culture and contemporary elegance, and, all over the world, crowds flocked to get a glimpse of her. Jackie was an exemplary First Lady, but, like Diana, she found her greatest pleasure in her children.

A lifelong admirer, Princess Diana once wrote a letter to Jackie's grown children, Caroline and John Jr., expressing how much their mother had served as her role model when it came to raising William and Harry in the public eye. (Diana did not live to see John Jr. and his wife die in a plane crash in 1999.)

During a brief trip to Cape Cod, I made a point to visit the Kennedy Museum in Hyannis Port, where I saw two little old ladies staring at a bronze statue of John and John Jr. entitled *What Could Have Been*. "They were two of handsomest men to have walked the face the earth," I overheard one old lady say to the other. I found myself nodding in agreement.

For too many archetypal women, they are blessed with "fairy tale" lives that ultimately end in tragedy. Eva Perón died of womb cancer, Diana and Grace were killed in car accidents, and Jackie lost both her husband and later her son in horrific circumstances. All these stories would require extensive rewriting to make marrying "a prince" a recipe for happily ever after.

But we don't love these women despite this. We love these women because of this. It is their elegance and strength in the face of hardship that defines their archetype; their elegance and strength that generates their universal power.

Jackie differed from the other women mentioned here in that she didn't die young—her husband did. We didn't mourn for her but with her. And, as the world tried to cope with the disorder and disbelief that followed the murder of JFK, Jackie rose to the challenge of letting the nation mourn *through* her. During this time of collective pain that united the country, it was Jackie's regal dignity and quiet grace that made her worthy of Arthurian legend.

After her husband's death, Jackie went on to work as an editor at Viking and Doubleday publishing houses. One of her most beloved projects was *The Power of Myth*, a book based on the teachings of renowned mythologist Joseph Campbell. Jackie, a living archetypal princess who became immortalized as the "Queen of Camelot," could easily have authored her own chapter.

Evita

* * *

She's a diamond in their dull gray lives.
And that's the hardest kind of stone.
It usually survives.

– FROM THE MUSICAL *EVITA* (1996)

I HAVE FOND MEMORIES of hitting the dance floor in college, belting out the words to Madonna's "Don't Cry for Me Argentina" techno remix. (When I bought the CD and listened to the track on repeat, my roommate was annoyed but more than thankful that I was no longer playing Disney Princess songs.)

Before that time, I hadn't been truly aware of Eva Perón (a.k.a. Evita) and her story, but the hype surrounding the movie made me research further, and soon I became absolutely fascinated by this amazing woman who seemed to be a princess in everything but title.

Young Eva Duarte was an aspiring actress born into obscure poverty, but as per her royal archetype, her determination and sense of destiny allowed her to rise quickly. Eva married Colonel Juan Perón in 1942, and two years later he became president of

Argentina. Evita served as his First Lady for eight years, eventually wielding more power and influence than any woman in the history of Latin America.

Even more beautiful and charismatic than Madonna (who portrayed her in the 1996 musical biopic), Evita became a truly international figure and worldwide topic of conversation. She was a huge champion of women's suffrage and eventually founded Argentina's first large-scale female political party. She set up offices in the Ministry of Labor and Social Welfare, holding daily audiences and distributing food and medicine to the underprivileged. Evita was always at her husband's side, and, quite controversially, they ran the country as a team.

Like all archetypal princesses, Evita Perón achieved untold popularity and adoration by presenting the public with a living image of their own dreams. Just like Jackie Kennedy, Evita's appeal transcended politics. Just like Princess Diana, Evita was a rebel within the establishment—but, knowing she was the key to their newfound popularity, they couldn't do a thing about it. Also like Diana, Evita's mix of stylish elegance and social conscience captured the hearts of the masses. Sadly, just like Diana, Evita died young (age 33) and the fairy tale that is her legacy lives on. In the years following Eva Perón's death, the Vatican received more than 40,000 letters attributing to her various miracles and urging that she be declared a saint.

She did not wear a crown, but what made Evita a true archetypal princess is that she showed the world how a woman could possess both femininity *and* power—and how, in fact, the two went hand in hand.

Kate

. . .

He's lucky to be going out with me.

— KATE MIDDLETON, WHEN ASKED HOW SHE FELT
TO BE DATING PRINCE WILLIAM

Her ponytail made me want to be a better person.

— REPORTER JOSH DUBOFF, WHEN DESCRIBING HIS
ENCOUNTER WITH KATE IN *VANITY FAIR*

I REALIZE THE VERY concept of a class system can be hard for most Americans to grasp—after all, it's been drummed into our heads since birth that all people are created equal. But class pervades every single aspect of English life. Within moments, Brits can easily categorize others as upper class, middle-upper class, upper-middle class, middle-middle class, lower-middle, upper-lower, middle-lower, and so on based on activities as simple as drinking tea. A desire to advance one's social and economic standing is what the American dream is based on, but in the UK, upward mobility of any kind can cause mockery and distrust.

This is why Kate Middleton is so revolutionary. She is known as HRH the Duchess of Cambridge, but she is technically a princess.[11] More than that, she is a *middle-class* princess with *working-class* roots (her great-grandfather was a coal miner), which, in one of the most classist societies on Earth, is *huge*. Not since King Edward IV's controversial marriage to widowed commoner Elizabeth Woodville (a.k.a. *The White Queen*) has such a seditious royal match transpired.

Historically, royal marriages were about creating or bolstering alliances with foreign powers, but Kate and William's love story provides something even more important for royals in the twenty-first century: an alliance with the British people.

Kate is clearly intelligent, and will be the first British Queen with a university degree. But she's also shown women of the world that they should never be intimidated by someone others may view as out of their league. Even if that is all she ever does, Kate's very presence on the balcony of Buckingham Palace has shown ordinary women that they too are worthy of a royal crown—and in many ways, that is enough.

Although Kate has become a bigger box office pull than the rest of her in-laws combined, she is changing the very face of celebrity by injecting it with restraint; while others have clamored to confess all, she maintains a regal silence. ("Minimum information given with maximum politeness" was Jackie Kennedy's media strategy, and Kate seems to have borrowed it beautifully.) In an age of Kardashians and *Real Housewives*, this is radical stuff.

Yes, Kate married into her royal position. And some have labeled her weak and submissive because she waited around for that balding prince to propose, even though she happened to be in love with him. But Kate has shown us that life as a princess doesn't have to mean condemning oneself to a miserable existence with a heartless husband; because, as William stands proudly at her side, Kate has shown us that a princess can also be loved.

"Of course I want my daughter to hope for more than 'marrying well,'" said a friend of mine when I asked her about America's love affair with Kate (who has appeared on more than three hundred US magazine covers since her engagement). "But I also hope that I can teach her the importance of a healthy relationship and happy marriage. And I think William and Kate are great role models for this. My daughter doesn't have to believe in fairy tales. But I do want her to believe in happiness."

If Kate lacks an edge over the other women listed here, it is because her life lacks suffering. But William's life most certainly does not, and Kate's quiet strength will become integral to William's role as the years go on.

Let us remember that the UK government, like most Western governments, is predominately, overwhelmingly, male; as I write this there are only *four women* in Parliament's front benches. Thankfully, Queen Elizabeth II provides a formidable female force to balance things out, albeit symbolically. But when the Queen dies and Prince Charles inherits the throne, it will become glaringly obvious how male dominated the UK power structure really is. This is when Kate will come into her own—when she finds herself as the young matriarch, the beautiful female figurehead, among a sea of men in gray suits.

And so to Kate's critics, who insist that accepting her role as a princess has done no favors for womankind—the joke is on them. Because over the next half century, The Duchess of Cambridge will be able to wield more power, however subtly, than any of her elected male counterparts. She will have more global influence over an entire generation and more access to powerful decision makers than most men only dream about.

When William is King, I predict his reign will become a co-regency in everything but name and Kate will become the shining sun around which the entire monarchy revolves. Because she keeps so much to herself, Kate may not be as emotionally satisfying as Diana, but as she settles into her new position, let us hope she finds a purpose, and a voice, beyond what is expected of her.

She will be the country's sixth Queen Catherine. But with increasing wisdom and grace, perhaps she will go down in history as none other than "Kate the Great."

ON MAY 2, 2015, Kate gave birth to her second child, Princess Charlotte Elizabeth Diana of Cambridge. And the infant princess made history the moment she was born. With the UK's newly enshrined Succession to the Crown Act, Princess Charlotte will be fourth in line to the British throne—and, for the first time in the monarchy's history, any younger brothers will not be allowed to supersede her. It's not a huge win for feminism, but in a world where millions of girls are undervalued, it is a small yet significant change to the status of women.

Princess Charlotte may be royal, but she is still a female, and, like all girls, she will have to navigate what that means in the twenty-first century. Some predict that Charlotte, no matter what she does, will be endlessly photographed, gawked at, gossiped about, and viewed as a clotheshorse and/or a soap opera character.

They're probably right.

But as we watch Princess Diana's granddaughter grow up, let's hope she inherits her grandmother's spirit and courage. Let's hope she doesn't care whether her behavior is deemed "unfeminine," but, in the same vein, let's hope she is not made to feel inferior if "girly" or "ladylike" is what she wants to be. Like all little girls, let's hope she doesn't grow up to be rude or unkind yet never feels restricted by her gender or her title.

And, finally, let us hope that with Kate's guidance, Princess Charlotte will learn to be generous with her power. May she learn to use her privileged position, her public role, and her odd fairytale existence not simply to amuse or adorn but to increase the well-being of her realm and to do genuine, lasting good.

Chapter V

IN DEFENSE OF
BEAUTY

. . . . .

Women's lives are multilayered;
I have no problem understanding that women can
be interested in mascara and the Middle East.

– JOANNA COLES, EDITOR IN CHIEF OF *COSMOPOLITAN*

A s I MENTIONED BEFORE, what my mother deemed acceptable television viewing material when I was child was very slim indeed. This caused many a heated battle in my household because while I was relatively okay with not being able to watch a large quantity of television, the single TV program I was dying to see was completely taboo.

As far as I could tell, aside from my town's homecoming queen contest, the Miss America Pageant was all my country had that vaguely resembled any kind of royalty—and because of this I would strategically plan sleepovers at my best friend's house in order to watch the live broadcast every single year. I loved the royal sashes, the princessy evening gowns, the long white gloves, and the giant rhinestone tiaras. I loved the zany talents and the heartfelt interviews. And I loved the ending when the crowned winner inevitably cried through her not entirely waterproof mascara.

My friend Chelsea and I used to keep complicated scoring charts in which we'd judge every contestant in each competition according to our very strict criteria. And when it came to our ten-year-old comments, let me tell you, Simon Cowell had nothing on us.

Year after year, my mom railed against these pageants—disgusted at the objectification of women and how decades after the dawn of American feminism, women were still being judged on how they looked in a swimsuit. Year after year, I kept championing the pageants' good qualities: the talent competition, the charity platform, the college scholarships. Middle school came and went, junior high school came and went—yet this petty fight over beauty pageants continued to flare up in our household.

Despite my 4.0 GPA, I didn't play a varsity sport and therefore did not possess the only criterion required to be in the running for junior homecoming queen. (And I ask you: What kind of message is *that* to send to young girls?) Yet I remained so incredibly fascinated by the princess-like world of pageants that, when I turned fourteen, I researched one that was being held in Colorado and entered it.

My mother was horrified. But, after countless high-volume debates, she agreed to let me do it—under the condition that she was not going to give me one penny toward the cost. I was not daunted. I knocked on the door of every business in my community, showed them my flawless academic record, and politely asked for sponsorship. Some knew my mother, and many even agreed with her views, but, once I presented my case and explained how I'd love to represent the magnificent state of Colorado, I never walked away empty handed. It was quite a crash course in fundraising, but I ended up with enough money for the $500 entrance fee, my evening dress, my interview suit, and three nights of accommodation in Denver. I've never been the singing/dancing type, so I elected to enter the speech competition instead of the talent show, and I invited all of my relatives to the event (all of whom accepted on the spot, fascinated by the mother-daughter battle for women's rights that would be happening on stage).

I practiced walking in heels beneath the massive skirt of my puffy satin ball dress (which I chose because the neckline resembled Sleeping Beauty's), I prepped for my interview, and I wrote quite a cheesy and inspiring speech entitled "Youth: Pride of the Present, Hope of the Future." Then I packed my family up in the old station wagon, and my dad drove us to Denver.

I'm not quite sure what I expected to find at that pageant—lots of girls like me, maybe? Girls like Erin Brockovich? Girls who craved royal adventure as much as I did? Girls who were as serious about college as they were about tiaras? I don't know, really. All I know is that, once I entered that Denver Hyatt Hotel, I didn't find any of that.

To me, that pageant was always just a small summer stepping stone to something greater. (I planned to get accepted to an Ivy League school then move to Europe and be a *real* princess, remember?) But most of the girls I encountered at that pageant were either depressingly indifferent to the entire experience or freakishly excited about it. No one really seemed to be taking the whole grace and poise part seriously, and all anyone could really talk about was the extortionate cost of it all. No one appeared to have genuine career goals beyond becoming a flight attendant, and no one seemed interested in traveling beyond Orlando, Florida, in her lifetime. But it was too late to admit this to anyone. Much like the girl in *Little Miss Sunshine*, I had already dragged my whole family halfway across the state, and my entire extended family had tickets to that evening's gala performance.

And yet my mom never said a word. She helped me get everywhere on time and told me not to worry when I flubbed my interview by not being able to remember the Colorado state bird. (Just so you know, it's the lark bunting.) She was wonderful. But I think she knew that I was seeing the pageant world for what it really was and that, somewhere in all of this, I was learning my lesson.

As I sat backstage before the pageant began, I overheard two previous pageant winners giggling to each other about their plans for getting drunk that night. They were fifteen years old. Until then, I had admired these girls whose triumphant faces graced the glossy pageant brochures, but, in that moment, the spell was broken. Pageants were not the path to princesshood. And I was mortified that I'd ever thought as much.

I went through the motions of the pageant. Wearing our requisite white dresses, I did my dance routine with the other girls ("You looked like a bunch of crazy nurses," my little brother told me), I smiled till my face hurt, and I won Best Speech (which bizarrely meant half as much prize money as the cash award for Miss Photogenic).

That night, with my beautiful Sleeping Beauty ball gown and my bouncy Rapunzel hair, I'm sure I looked like a princess. But, in my heart, I didn't feel like one. That night, the crown for wisdom went to my bra-burning mother.

ROYAL BEAUTY

. . .

WHEN KATE MIDDLETON TRAVELED to Harlem's Northside Center for Child Development in December 2014, many of the children there were surprised that she did not resemble Elsa from *Frozen*. We merely have to observe current photos of Princess Anne beside photos of Charlene of Monaco to see that although an element of glamour helps get the job done, it's by no means necessary to fulfill a royal role.

And if the pasty, bug-eyed portraits of the young Princess Victoria and Catherine of Aragon (who was a Spanish princess before she married Henry VIII) are anything to go by—it's clear that ideas about royal beauty have changed over the years and are largely dependent on trends of the era. (More than anything else, Princess Victoria was worried that her hands were too large.)

Cinderella, whose film was released in 1950, has definite shades of a certain screen siren named Grace Kelly, who made her feature debut that same year. Princess Aurora's character in *Sleeping Beauty* holds more than a passing resemblance to a popular new doll named Barbie—both of which launched in 1959. All the animated princesses seem to walk through life with the regal grace found in classical dance—because their movements were modeled on actual ballet dancers.

Whereas, in previous centuries, small eyes and rosebud mouths were the ideal, with the advent of cameras, large photogenic eyes have become the new norm, and this is reflected in the modern Disney princesses. Some complain that Disney's princesses have unrealistic waist measurements, but I'm afraid that cartoons are not meant to be photo-realistic. (Does anyone complain that Charlie Brown's head is twice the size of his body?)

Many think that fairytale princesses propagate the notion that beautiful means good and ugly means bad, but this is far from true. In the Grimms' version of *Cinderella*, the stepsisters are not ugly; they are "beautiful and fair of face, but vile and black of heart." In *Beauty and the Beast*, the central curse only occurs because the vain prince cannot offer kindness to a hideous beggar woman who is really an elegant enchantress in disguise. Likewise, the principal theme in *The Frog Prince* is that we mustn't judge others based on appearance; be kind to all beings (even repulsive reptiles), as you never know what inner beauty lies beneath the surface.

So, just as women should never be judged by how they dress, even if they're wearing a miniskirt, princesses should never be dismissed for how they look, even if they are beautiful.

PRETTY, PRETTY PRINCESS

. . .

FAIRY TALES HAVE ALWAYS been about transformation, and the magic found in what we now call a "makeover" is part of this tradition. *Glamour* is actually an ancient Scottish word meaning "magical spell."

Whether in *Frozen*, *Cinderella*, or even Hollywood remakes of Cinderella like *My Fair Lady*, *Pretty Woman*, and *Legally Blonde*, the mythical power of a fairytale makeover isn't just about changing one's external appearance. The magic actually hinges on the idea that a woman's outer beauty is dependent upon the revelation of her *inner* beauty.

"This is why," Justine Musk explains, "we'll often signal a dramatic change in our ongoing life story (such as divorce) with an equally dramatic haircut. Women understand that transformation often happens from the outside in."[1]

Peggy Orenstein counters this directly: "What I am exploring [in *Cinderella Ate My Daughter*] is the unprecedented marketing to girls at ever-earlier ages that encourages them to define themselves through appearance and play sexiness. And the ways that they learn to see their femininity, sexuality, and identity from the outside in rather from the inside out. How the princesses are currently marketed plays into that flume ride."[2]

I've read Orenstein's book cover to cover. (I had to find out why she was so critical of my favorite fictional ladies.) And although a lot of her book made me growl with annoyance, I have to admit I found much of it to be endearingly familiar—mainly because Orenstein's thought process reminds me so much of my own mother's. In that sense, I totally understand the love-fueled desire of intelligent women to fiercely protect their daughters from anything and everything in life that might be detrimental. And I truly believe that this parenting approach comes from the deepest and most genuine love.

But do princesses really reinforce the idea that a woman's primary purpose is to be decorative? Only if you think women can't simultaneously be well-dressed, intelligent, *and* really good at what they do. Do princesses really prompt early sexualization? I think that's a stretch.

"I love the Disney princesses," one mother told me. "Unlike real actresses, I don't have to worry about my daughter going online and finding the lost sex tapes of Snow White or Belle's topless photo shoot from before she was famous."

I'm not going to pretend that appearance has no connection to the princess genre, but Disney princesses are hardly posing for *Playboy* or rushing to second base. They don't dream of hook-ups and one-night stands; they dream of finding true and lasting love. And banning all princesses in an attempt to police early sexuality has a dangerous crossover with policing femininity.

Besides, if we look closely, you'll see that the princess stories have always focused on inner qualities rather than outward appearance. Even in *The Little Mermaid* (the princess story everyone loves to hate), Ariel's voice is considered more powerful and more valuable than her beauty—yet this metaphorical detail is routinely ignored.

Faran Krentcil writes in *Elle* magazine that if adults project too much fear and anxiety on the beauty of the Disney princesses, we end up inadvertently promoting "a damaging either/or school of girlhood with constraints like 'the pretty one' or 'the smart one.'

"And it's those either/or labels," she argues, "not Princess Culture—that are really wrecking our young women's confidence."[3]

I will concede that while Disney princess movies carry positive messaging, it's not at all helpful when the corresponding merchandise doesn't reflect these same ideas. A recent study found that 31 percent of "girl" toys are about appearance, and I categorically believe that is wrong.[4] (Personally, I'm still waiting for a *Beauty and Beast*–themed library set to be released. Maybe a chess board from *Tangled* or a trade agreement kit from *Frozen's* Kingdom of Arendelle . . .)

However, even if little girls weren't bombarded with endless appearance-related merchandise; most adults are guilty of constantly telling little girls how pretty they are. (We all do it; it's human nature. We can't stop ourselves complimenting an adorable child any more than we can stop ourselves from going gaga over a brand new puppy.)

It may be impossible for us to completely prevent girls from being exposed to ideas about beauty we disagree with, but it is possible for us to manage how these ideas might affect them. So if we're serious about instilling strong self-esteem in our girls, these are the regal rules:

1. Don't talk (or worry incessantly) about how pretty the princesses are.
2. Don't ever mention diets or weight gain.
3. Don't ever criticize other women.
4. Don't talk excessively about your daughter's beauty or your own.
5. *Do* tell her that you love her. All the time.

MOTHERING INFLUENCE

. . .

DECADES BEFORE IT BECAME trendy, my parents were obsessed with healthy eating. I was raised a vegetarian, occasionally allowed fish, and never allowed to consume anything processed or artificial. Snacking didn't happen, chemicals and refined sugar were banned, tofu was a staple, and salad was served with every single meal. If I wanted a dessert, I had to ask specifically for the ingredients required to bake it myself. My parents *never* mentioned the idea of gaining weight in front of me. It was such a nonissue in my house that as a teenager, the concept literally never even occurred to me.

Likewise, issues of body image never arose because they didn't need to. My parents knew I was healthy and confident and if I wanted to spend my allowance on *Vogue* magazine and devour every supermodel-filled page, they weren't worried. If I wanted to wear short skirts to school every day, they weren't going to stop me. They knew I had zero interest in the boys at school because I told them all the time that I was saving myself for an English prince. (At this stage, my prince fantasy was ideal since it wasn't interfering with my life or education in the way real sex with a real boyfriend might have.)

It was only when I arrived at college and was confronted with nightly beer fests and the all-you-can-eat buffets that I noticed my body shape changing. (At first, I was certain I'd shrunk all my jeans in the college dryers—that's how oblivious I was to the idea of weight gain.) But, despite my growing thighs and chubbier face, *it never occurred to me* that I was suddenly less likable or could be less successful. Thanks to my parents, my self-worth was not tied to these ideas.

I'm so saddened when I meet women in their twenties, thirties, even forties, whose mothers still regularly comment on their daughter's weight—always remarking whether she has or hasn't gained a few pounds. I see how this casual, maternal disapproval affects them far more than any animated princess or airbrushed supermodel ever could.

"Moms are the single most important influence on a daughter's body image," said Dr. Leslie Sim, child psychologist and clinical director of the Mayo Clinic's eating disorders program.[5]

So be a fairy godmother and use this influence. Stop obsessing about how unrealistically pretty the princesses may seem, and start turning princess play into something empowering.

There are countless ways of doing this. Start by making sure that when she puts on her princess persona that she is accessing her *inner* princess. Make her understand that a princess is more than just a dress or hairstyle—it is about kindness and compassion. Ask her often whether a real princess would do or say that. Learn the princess narratives—Disney and otherwise—for yourself, so that as an adult you can easily reference things that will help her princess make-believe to be about adventure, leadership, and benevolence. Learn about real and historical princesses so you can talk about new countries and cultures, diplomacy and philanthropy, duty and service.

Peggy Orenstein actually admitted, "It's not the Princesses that really bother me. . . . They're just a trigger for the bigger question of how I can help my daughter with the contradictions she will inevitably face as a girl, the dissonance that is as endemic as ever to growing up female."[6]

I have a daughter too. Raising her in this misogynistic world is terrifying. I get that. But, while we slowly battle the dragons of the patriarchy, there are other things we can do.

Talk about how the Disney princesses aren't afraid to speak their minds. Discuss how Princess Diana refused to sit quietly in her palace and instead forged ahead with her controversial charity work. Use these examples to encourage girls to speak up in class, to state their opinions, and be ready and willing to defend them. Talk about how real princesses don't always live happily ever after. (At least two died in car crashes—so always remember to wear your seat belt!)

Talk about how most of us in the Western world live more comfortably than fairytale princesses from medieval times ever did. Discuss how, even today, most real castles don't have electricity, heating, or running water. Discuss how we have better doctors, healthier food, and beds so soft that they were designed by NASA scientists. (Princess and the Pea, anyone?) Talk to girls about how pampered they already are compared to most of the world and how, in reality, they *already* live like royalty.

When she puts on that tiara, say this: "You're a princess? That's wonderful! Now, how are you going to solve the problems of your kingdom?"

No matter what your view toward princesses may be, it's amazingly easy to turn the princess obsession on its head and make it about so much more than simply looking pretty.

Cinderella was able to cope with the adversity of her situation while retaining her self-worth because her parents provided her with the foundation to do so. There is no reason we cannot strive to do the same.

WOMEN CAN HAVE IT ALL (EXCEPT FOR BEAUTY)

. . .

ALTHOUGH I WAS OBSESSED with Snow White as a young girl, her appearance never really came into it. Never once did I desire hair black as ebony or lips as red as blood. I simply wanted to *be* her—not look like her.

Yet one of the biggest criticisms continually aimed at the princess genre is that it seems to *celebrate* beauty. But what's wrong with that? Can't a woman be powerful, kind, and beautiful all at once?

If you were a man, you would honor *all* your strengths and talents—whatever they may be. Why can't women do the same? Women's biggest trump cards are too often dismissed, declared not only worthless but somehow foolish.

Justine Musk points out how women constantly belittle this part of themselves: "What's the one thing a woman can say that will ensure she gets absolutely massacred? 'I'm beautiful.' Even supermodels, who make fortunes off their looks, will tell stories about what ugly ducklings they were growing up, [forever downplaying their natural gift]."[7]

Think of Helen of Troy (also a princess). Nearly three millennia have passed, and she still has not been forgiven for the face she was born with, just because it happened to launch a thousand ships. Perhaps part of the problem is that most strong women are also proud women—and, for women, pride is often mistaken for vanity.

Marissa Mayer, CEO of Yahoo, took a huge bashing when she dared to pose for *Vogue*. But so what if she loves fashion? Do we think less of Larry Ellison for being photographed with his giant power boat or Richard Branson with his hot air balloons? Why are fashion and beauty always considered frivolous while more masculine hobbies are viewed as perfectly acceptable diversions?

"Men are allowed to talk about sports relentlessly," complains Joanna Coles, editor in chief of *Cosmopolitan* magazine, "and yet we still take them seriously. I don't understand why women can't talk about fashion . . . and not be taken as seriously as men."[8]

I would understand this hostility toward fashion and beauty if you assume women dress only to impress men and if you assume that women are incapable of simultaneously maintaining their appearance, holding down a career, and discussing world politics.

But if you don't assume these things? I don't understand what all the fuss is about.

The criticism aimed at former Texas senator Wendy Davis is another case in point. Davis is an incredible advocate for women's rights, but, because she has blond hair and perfect, southern grooming, her opponents immediately held it against her by calling her "Barbie"—as if being attractive and polished automatically made her as brainless as a plastic doll.

And, speaking of Barbie, here we have an unmarried, independent woman without children—a true feminist icon for those who fought against the domestic drudgery of the 1950s. But, like most princesses, Barbie seems to find that, no matter how much she achieves (she's had 150 careers and counting), people won't stop talking about her looks.

"The great irony of the Barbie debate," observes Charlotte Alter in *Time* magazine, "is that we spend so much time talking about how she looks and so little time talking about her careers. . . . Barbie represents beauty and materialism, but she also represents mutability, imagination and professional possibilities. If we took her work life half as seriously as we took her waist measurement, we could use Barbie as a way to talk to girls about the jobs they want, not the bodies they want."[9]

Speaking of waist measurements, rather than praising the tremendous strength of character actress Lily James brought to the role of Disney's live action *Cinderella* (she actually studied the teachings of Gandhi to prepare for the movie), all the critics could focus on was the size of her waist. At one point, the BBC News website listed more real-time views on this subject than the horrific fatal attacks that had happened that same day in Yemen.

It's ridiculous.

No one would dare to discuss Hillary Clinton's or Angela Merkel's waistlines to such an extent—because, with them, we should be focusing on what they're doing and saying rather than how they look.[10]

But shouldn't *all* women be judged on what they're doing and saying rather than how they look? Whatever happened to all the trendy feminist hash tags like #ViewsNotShoes and #AskHerMore? Why does none of this apply to Cinderella? Why are princesses always immune to these basic feminist rules? The hypocrisy of it astounds me.

Rather than discussing Cinderella's character, all the media could talk about was *her body*. Was her waistline photoshopped, or was it the corset in her costume? Did Lily James diet, or is she naturally that slender? When reading film reviews, one would think the plotline of the story, the quality of the script, and the talent of the cast depended entirely on these details.

Sandy Powell, *Cinderella*'s Oscar-winning costume designer, pointed out that no one makes a fuss when you see women wearing corsets in historical dramas. So why is a historical fairy tale any different?

Cinderella (or any woman for that matter) doesn't have to be wearing a shapeless sack to be a positive role model for girls. Surely what counts is her *behavior*. Is she a good person? Does she work hard? Is she true to herself?

Throughout the movie, Cinderella's motto is this: "have courage and be kind." Does her pretty blue dress totally negate the incredible power of these words?

I hope not.

Just as all women are a great deal more than pretty faces, princesses are a great deal more than small waists. Let's not lose sight of that.

WE ARE ALLOWED TO BE BEAUTIFUL

. . .

ON A BASIC, EVOLUTIONARY level, "good looks" tell us whether a person is potentially fertile, healthy, and strong and whether he or she might have genes that combine well with ours to make healthy babies. Princesses didn't engineer this concept—Darwin did.

For nearly 2,000 years, women were widely considered to be nothing more than men's property, and sensible women sought security by seeking the man best able to look after her and her children. Considering that men are highly visual creatures, for thousands of years, a woman's survival depended heavily on her appearance. Yes, times have changed—and thank God that they have. But the primal desire to attract the best mate in order to protect our offspring is still alive and well.

I'm not saying for one single second that women should believe their only source of value is their appearance, but it's fair to say that princesses (Disney or otherwise) are not wholly responsible for our society's obsession with beauty.

All cultures are beauty cultures. Every civilization reveres it and pursues it in its own way. Of course our bodies are worthy of love in their natural state, but the pleasures found in adornment are nothing new; the Egyptians had most of the same cosmetics we have today, which suggests that beauty behavior is hardly a response to current cultural pressures. Our beauty ideals have changed drastically over the years, but our desire to obtain beauty remains as strong as ever.

In her amazing book *Wonder Women: Sex, Power, and the Quest for Perfection*, President of Barnard College Debora Spar asks, "Are we really all just succumbing to male corporate manipulation? Or are we hostages to something deeper and more primitive within ourselves? . . . Maybe at some level and for some women, beauty *is* power . . . And maybe we're simply programmed, like preening peacocks, to polish and strut our stuff."[11]

For many women, beauty is not only a unique avenue of power but a unique avenue for feminine expression—neither of which should automatically be linked to attracting men, because both bring pleasure to women in their own right.

This said, the constant railing against the "beauty" of the princess genre, and the feminine expression that comes with it, is misplaced. The idea that Disney princesses or girls pretending to be princesses, or women who pursue feminine beauty and enjoy feminine fashion, are automatically dressing to attract male attention, rather than for their own enjoyment, is one of the biggest beauty myths of all. The fact that something appeals to the male gaze does not mean that it exists for the male gaze.

As grown women, why should we stop wearing things we might love (like dresses and high heels) in order to cater to what we think is everyone else's sexism? We are currently in the midst of a ubiquitous rape culture that wants us to believe women who wear makeup or short skirts deserve to be sexually assaulted. In this context, it's not very helpful to also say that women (princesses included) who dress and adorn themselves in a traditionally feminine way don't deserve to be taken seriously.

Eat, Pray, Love author Elizabeth Gilbert said recently, "No decision that any of us make about our appearance makes us morally better or morally worse than any other woman."[12]

This is especially true when we consider that the ways modern women interpret beauty cover an enormous range. On one hand, we have women who think any visual enhancement whatsoever is cowering to the patriarchy; that any hint of adornment is automatically giving in to a male marketing machine that makes women feel bad about themselves so they will continue to buy products they don't need. On the other hand, we have women who spend their entire lives crafting, sculpting, and surgically enhancing their bodies into their idea of perfection. Others simply see fashion as an art form, good grooming as good manners, and makeup as essential armor to face the day with confidence. But all women (wherever they fall on the spectrum) are doing the best they can to feel powerful and happy when they walk out the door.

Some fail to find or attain their personal definition of beauty, but many succeed. And in the midst of these mixed messages about what is and isn't appropriately beautiful or feminine, the last thing women should be doing is turning on each other (animated or otherwise).

I recently saw an incredible poster on the London underground advertising an upcoming exhibit at the Design Museum. In giant font it simply read: *Women, Fashion, Power: Not a Multiple Choice.*

I love this. It implies that, yes, these concepts are complicated and intertwined—but you know what? They don't require any disentanglement.

Women are multifaceted. So are princesses. That's what makes all of us so enchanting.

And though we don't have to be perfect, let's be crystal clear about one thing: we are allowed to be beautiful.

Chapter VI

IN DEFENSE OF REAL
ROYAL WOMEN

· · · · ·

*Even if you brought Clark Gable and Marilyn
Monroe back to life, America couldn't be more
excited than they are by the Cambridges.*

– STEPHEN FRY

MOST YOUNG GIRLS ARE told that the princess dream is something they must, and eventually will, grow out of. But we don't grow out of it, of course. We simply carry the secret princess longing into adulthood. And we all know if you have any kind of desire and you stifle it, it will consume you.

It's only when a bona fide royal wedding is announced that we allow ourselves to openly indulge our princess passions—but usually the princess dream has been repressed for so long that our global reaction borders on hysteria. Exhibit A: Diana Spencer's wedding to Prince Charles; Exhibit B: Kate Middleton's wedding to Prince William.

The British royal family dates back to AD 400. Yet the media furor surrounding Kate and William's fairytale wedding in 2011 showed quite clearly that the idea of a royal family still captures our hearts in the twenty-first century. It doesn't matter whether the words "fairytale wedding" make you nauseous or whether you find the idea of a monarchy completely offensive to your democratic sensibilities. The fact is that fairy tales, even if they are socially constructed, still wield an incredible power over us all.

When I made it known that I was throwing a party to celebrate the royal wedding (dress code: Westminster Abbey chic), one by one, women came forward, shyly asking whether they could come along. These were savvy, intelligent women who wouldn't be caught dead reading *People* magazine because when they go to the hairdresser they bring their own copy of the *Economist*.

In the beginning, they made it clear to me that their interest in the royal wedding was under the guise of apathy or humor: "it's so tacky and vulgar that I might as well watch it," or "I only want to see her dress," or "can I bring my guillotine?"

But despite what I'm sure they thought were very "feminist" rationales, on the wedding day itself, everyone was magically transformed into loyal monarchists. They adhered to my dress code (even their husbands wore tailcoats!), drank mimosas, and munched on scones. And there wasn't a dry eye in the house.

For there, on the television screen, was an ordinary girl who never gave up on love. Her princess dream was coming true, not just symbolically but literally. And beside her was the lanky blond boy who, not that long ago, broke our hearts as he walked stoically behind his mother's coffin. Love is powerful and so are fairy tales. And if that wedding taught us anything that day, it was that, deep down, everyone still believed in both.

One of my best British friends had recently relocated to Silicon Valley, and she thought hosting a royal wedding party would be a great way to meet her new American neighbors. She was right. The Americans turned up in droves to drink Earl Grey (how British!) and see the BBC wedding coverage projected on her living room wall.

"But I didn't really get to know anyone," my friend complained to me. "No one wanted to mingle or talk. They really just wanted to watch every detail of the wedding! They sat in silence for nearly two hours!"

I wasn't surprised.

The unconscious, collective urge for a happy ending is intoxicating.

And the chance to participate in such an archetypal fairy tale was irresistible for most of the planet.

Still, it's quite impossible to imagine billions of people bothering to watch the wedding of an elected president's grandson (much less the funeral of an elected president's former daughter-in-law). But if the elected president is a *Queen?* Things are different.

For whatever reason, real royalty changes things. Real royalty makes us care.

THE POWER OF DYNASTIES

• • •

I KNOW THAT MY equality-loving parents (who, for several years before I was born, did not believe in money) were slightly disturbed by my incessant girlhood passion for princesses. Fairy tales were one thing, but in my parents' eyes, real princesses were part of an ancient, nondemocratic form of government and part of a regressive class system—both of which represented all the trappings of material wealth they had spent most of the late 1960s actively rejecting.

But they forgot to factor in one thing: royalty is *romantic*. And, for better or for worse, America's monarchy-free government lacks this distinctive allure.

My memoir was entitled *Someday My Prince Will Come*. Quite frankly, I'm not sure I would have gotten a book deal if my story was called *Someday My Undersecretary of the Interior Will Come*. No one is interested in that story. It's not romantic. The US cabinet is not the stuff of fairy tales and legend. It's not where enchanted folklore begins and ends. But royalty? Monarchy? *Real live princes walking the earth*? That's downright magical. Despite all our intellect telling us otherwise, how can we not get caught up by it?

Actress Marlo Thomas understands this obsession (and freely admits she loves a royal news story). Thomas observes that, "for all the revolutionary blood that was shed, Americans are in a perpetual state of Royal Envy. . . . After all, there are no carriages taking us to *our* weddings. No beefeaters guarding *our* houses."[1]

She has a point. You simply can't escape the fact that the Windsor dynasty, with all its regal glamour and enchantment, is a lot more interesting than American dynasties made up of Bushes or Clintons.

Yes, Britain's monarchy is hereditary and many can't stomach that concept. But if you really want to delve into the finer points of political science and compare systems of governments to see which is better or more democratic than the other, let's do it. Because if we are really truthful with ourselves, I would argue that America is no longer the perfect democratic republic envisioned by our Founding Fathers.

Increasingly, America has become a country led by a small dominant class of rich and powerful members who exert total control over the general population—and in political speak this is known as an *oligarchy*, which is basically just a monarchy without a king and queen. (Research attesting to this reality was found in a joint study by Princeton and Northwestern Universities, revealing that "the preferences of the average American appear to have only a minuscule, near-zero, statistically non-significant impact upon public policy."[2])

I hope this will change soon, but, as things stand, it's hard for me to be smug about how the American government is *soooo* much better than one that has a hereditary royal family.

So when Americans complain to me about elected politicians, I often joke that if the end result is the same, we might as well go with the more glamorous royal option—at least we'd have more pomp and pageantry to brighten our days.

As it stands, Americans "are extremely jealous of the British royal family," observes author Russ Baker, an expert on the Bush dynasty. "We like the idea of being able to rise up from nothing, but we are still hung up on status. . . . We still crave the fantasy of royalty."[3]

So it seems. For a nation that has constitutionally banned inherited power (the Constitution states quite clearly that "no title of nobility shall be granted by the United States"), we seem to feel quite comfortable with allowing political royalty to thrive.

The US was founded by rejecting all hereditary power, but before you knew it, the Adams family had two presidents. Throughout our nation's history, Americans have instinctively veered toward familiar names when electing our most powerful leaders. So far we've had the Adamses, the Harrisons, the Roosevelts, the Kennedys—and now, with the Bushes and the Clintons, it still seems that we can't think beyond more than two families when it comes to selecting someone to fill our highest office. Out of forty-four US presidents, eight of them hail from just four families. And more than 10 percent of the US Congress have had blood relatives enter Congress ahead of them. (Cities and states do it too: California had the Browns; Ohio had the Tafts; Chicago had the Daleys.) On top this, twelve-year-old BridgeAnne d'Avignon of California discovered that all US presidents (bar one) are directly descended from a single British monarch: King John of England, who signed the Magna Carta in 1215.[4]

"Perhaps human nature naturally craves a hereditary monarchy," suggests Satoshi Kanazawa in *Psychology Today*. "Why else would a representative democracy continually elect wives, sons, and other family members of politicians to succeed?"[5]

Author Tina Brown describes monarchy as a "golden thread that connects people to the most glorious moments in their history, exercising a force of stability in an otherwise bewildering changing world."[6]

This golden thread is what Americans lack, and, for better or worse, it is something we long for. Monarchies that are still in existence remain oddly irresistible to us. We love the fact that there are countries in the world where electric cars and glass coaches can coexist. We will happily fly across an ocean to see a land filled with palaces that aren't modeled after Disney cartoons—castles built hundreds of years ago that still belong to a living, breathing queen. Yes, the Palace of Versailles is gorgeous—but the Tower of London is far more magical to visitors because the royal crest on the yeomen warders' uniform is actually still applicable, not a historical re-enactment. What makes England such a fascinating and enchanted fairytale kingdom is precisely because it's part of a *real* kingdom.

REAL QUEENS

. . .

*When a true queen emerges she is magical
and enchanting; she is calm and she is happy.
She creates order where there was none.*

— MARIANNE WILLIAMSON

THE QUEEN OF ENGLAND is often referred to as the British *Sovereign*, and, like all queens, she is a living symbol of her subjects' collective power and the subconscious sovereignty that exists inside us all.

A special coin commemorating Queen Elizabeth II's fifty years on the throne was inscribed *Amor populi præsidium reg*: "The love of the people is the Queen's protection"—which is really all you need to know about the balance of power in modern Britain.

Born in 1926, the Queen is diplomacy personified; a constant symbol of hard work, dedication, and ability to weather the storm. In fact, Elizabeth II is so respected and beloved that many British people who would never refer to themselves as monarchists will quite happily call themselves "Queen-ists."

Distinguished British journalist and firm antimonarchist Jeremy Paxman was startled to his very core by the awed reaction he experienced when he bumped into Queen Elizabeth at a media reception. In a room packed with people famous for their intellect and power, he observed that in the Queen's presence, "the self-possessed became gauche and the eloquent were struck dumb"—and he was shocked to discover that when face to face with this "diminutive grandmother," he was no exception.[7]

A 1937 editorial in the *Times* of London explained that a successful monarch was dependent upon the "moral qualities of steadiness, staying power and self-sacrifice."[8] And, nearly a century later, these words still ring true. A British poll asking who provides the most moral leadership showed Queen Elizabeth II coming first, well ahead of the Archbishop of Canterbury—and both were comfortably ahead of the Prime Minister.

The Queen provides not only a connection to history, but also the greatest constancy most Brits have ever known. On September 9, 2015, Elizabeth II eclipsed Queen Victoria and became the UK's longest-serving monarch (reigning longer than all forty-one kings and queens of England since the Norman Conquest). Regardless of political feelings toward the monarchy, the British quietly rejoiced. Because for the last sixty-three years and seven months, they had shared Her Majesty's unifying blessing of "steadiness, staying power and self-sacrifice," and, whether or not they admit it, they still hold tight to her "golden thread" of security.

Yet some will continue to argue that royals should not be overly exalted or praised because they haven't actually earned their positions.

"You could argue that the Queen was 'born great,' and that the Duchess of Cambridge has had greatness 'thrust upon' her through marriage," said Sally Peck in the *Daily Telegraph*. "But when looking for female role models, we can do a lot worse than these two."[9]

Yes, Elizabeth was born a princess, and Kate became one through marriage, but let's think twice before assuming the means don't justify the end. Like the majority of females, I was born a woman, and I became a wife by marriage. The means by which I obtained these roles does not diminish their inherent value.

Think of powerful women like Melinda Gates or Michelle Obama who are using their influence to eradicate third world poverty and disease, to fight child obesity, help homeless veterans, and ensure all girls get the education they deserve. These are laudable activities that are creating real and positive change in the world. Does it really matter how these women obtained their leverage? Does it make their efforts and achievements less important?

And for those who bemoan the world's lack of female leaders, it's worth noting that until Queen Beatrix of the Netherlands retired in 2013, nearly half of Europe's reigning monarchs were women. On top of this, almost all of the royal families in Europe (including those of Norway, Spain, Sweden, Holland, and Belgium) have *female heirs*. In terms of lasting female influence on the geopolitical stage, this is hugely significant.

There have been thirty-four kings and only six queens in the course of the British monarchy's thousand-year history, and yet some of the country's most prosperous and enlightened times occurred during female reigns. Queen Elizabeth I ruled throughout the Golden Age, while Queen Victoria and Queen Elizabeth II boast the most progressive legacies of all time.

The first Queen Elizabeth (the all-conquering Tudor beauty portrayed by Cate Blanchett), was both a brilliant strategist and a beguiling woman. She famously used her unmarried status to send a powerful political message: there was no need for any man to marry her (and attempt to rule through her) because she was already "married to England." Elizabeth I and her ageless glamour gave form to the quintessential royal archetype in that she never compromised her femininity to achieve her political goals and obtain what was best for her kingdom.

Meanwhile, Queen Victoria used her role as a devoted wife and mother to become the symbolic wife and mother to her entire country. Her matriarchal presence during the chaos of the Industrial Revolution conveyed the vital message that Britain was still stable and strong. (And almost all current European monarchies are directly descended from Queen Victoria's nine children and/or twenty-six grandchildren.)

In this century, we have Queen Letizia of Spain. Once an award-winning television reporter, Letizia has worked for CNN, ABC, and Bloomberg, reporting from some of the world's most hostile environments. She covered the 2000 US presidential election, broadcast live from Ground Zero after the 2001 September 11 attacks, and reported from the front lines of the Iraq War. Letizia met Prince Felipe a year later when she was sent to northern Spain to cover the environmental wreckage caused by a sinking oil tanker. She was a divorcée (pass the smelling salts!)—but in the face of true love, this didn't matter. Queen Letizia now works closely with the Codespa Foundation (assisting poor communities with health, educational, and vocational training programs) and is the mother of two beautiful daughters. The eldest is Leonor, Spain's Hereditary Princess—which means there is more girl power to come.

Fluent in four languages, Queen Mathilde of Belgium was working as a speech therapist in her own practice when she met Prince Philippe. A mother of four, her eldest daughter Elisabeth was the first female in the Western world to have been born as heir apparent. In conjunction with UNICEF, Mathilde has presided over several humanitarian missions abroad, promoting children's rights and the empowerment of women. She's also worked as a United Nations envoy for the International Year on Microcredit and as a UNICEF special representative for their campaign to help children orphaned by HIV/AIDS.

Queen Maxima of the Netherlands (a mother of three) is hugely passionate about reducing global poverty through microfinance. Because of her expertise in the field (she was working as an investment banker when she met Prince Willem-Alexander), she was named the UN Special Advocate for Inclusive Finance for Development. Maxima's eldest daughter, Catharina-Amalia, is the Hereditary Princess of the Netherlands—so we have yet another female leader to look forward to.

Finally we have the indomitable Queen Rania of Jordan, who tirelessly campaigns for women's rights, economic fairness, and education reform. Also a mother of four, she continues to openly discuss formerly taboo topics like domestic violence, child abuse, and honor killings—serving as a hugely important role model for young girls and women in the Middle East.

Reading these short bios, I would be thrilled to one day be considered even half the woman these women are. I would be thrilled for my daughter to be considered even half the woman these women are.

But we mustn't forget: these women did not become queens overnight. Like all of us, they started out as princesses.

REAL PRINCESSES

· · ·

Reflexive disapproval of princesses is a bit passé.

– NAOMI WOLF

I AM CONSTANTLY BAFFLED as to why a real princess is always fair game for criticism, while, for the most part, real princes are left alone. Is an actress less worthy than an actor? A waiter more talented than a waitress? Of course not. You'd never dream of insinuating such things where other professions are concerned.

Whether a real prince or a real princess, both are this: young royals who are learning to become benevolent leaders. Male or female, they must learn to act gracefully, compassionately, and intelligently—all while growing into the kings and queens they are destined to be. Male or female, the value and challenge of the job description remains unchanged.

Besides, in this day and age, real princesses are not just ladies who lunch, dress well, and accept flowers. They don't simply cut ribbons, smile endlessly, and automatically defer to their husbands. That old stereotype couldn't be further from the truth. Real princesses, like all real women, defy clichés and categorization. And anyone attacking them on principle might as well attack all women on principle.

"The myth of the quiet, compliant wife is not corroborated by any 21st-century royal family," observes historian Marina Warner.[10]

She's right. Today, most real princesses have at least one college degree, if not several. Fluency in multiple languages is also the norm. And, like all modern young women, they knew perfectly well that they couldn't plan their life around a future husband so they forged careers in subjects in which they excelled. Be it journalism, advertising, or banking—the skills these women gleaned during their time in the business world (leadership, diplomacy, hard work) went on to serve them well in their future royal roles.

Now that they are officially crowned, these royal women have learned to look beyond themselves in every situation. While juggling the everyday demands of marriage and children, they must remember to place the well-being of their realm before all else. Yes, royal manners play a part in their daily life (they are experts in formal dining, know how to curtsey, and always—always—write thank you notes), but all princesses understand that traditional etiquette is not about being superior to others but about making those around you feel comfortable.

And as with all royal women throughout history, these ladies know that their custodial role is not a short-term game—it's one that requires patience and a plan for the future. Their respective monarchies cannot survive if these princesses don't maintain a carefully thought-out, long-term vision. (Wouldn't it be nice if bankers and members of congress did the same?)

Most of the world's real princesses hail from normal, hardworking families and don't have an ounce of blue blood running through their veins. But what they may lack in aristocratic breeding, they have made up for in self-belief. Long ago, these women learned to ignore their critics. They know they are worthy of a prince and don't let anyone tell them otherwise. And although critics refuse to believe it, all of them married for love.

Yes, royal marriages *used to be* about expanding power, wealth, and geographic clout, but that is no longer the case. Almost every contemporary crown prince in Europe has fallen in love with a commoner and, despite the historical precedent, chose to marry her anyway.

Let me come right out and say that I don't think any woman should be expected to give up her life to support her husband's role—unless she genuinely wants to. But potential princesses face an unusual challenge when they fall in love, because they don't just marry the man of their dreams, they marry into his bizarre family business. Princes also face an unusual challenge (William comes to mind), because, when they meet the girl of their dreams, they must ask her to *join* their bizarre family business. It must make for some difficult pillow talk.

For real royals, their love lives and their careers merge into one. It may be medieval and antiquated, but that's the way it works, and we should give them some credit for juggling their odd circumstances so beautifully.

And although many assume that royal men always have the upper hand, ordinary women wield more power than you think. After all, Edward VIII gave up his throne to marry Wallis Simpson; Henry VIII reshaped his nation's entire history to marry Anne Boleyn.

But, history aside, what's a *modern* girl to do? She finally falls in love, but, alas, her would-be husband comes with a built-in career track. Being a princess may not be something she ever imagined for herself, but perhaps she knows she'd be good at it, and perhaps she knows she might even enjoy it. Is she supposed to turn her back on true love because the arrangement is not entirely on her terms? All couples, royal or not, make compromises. But, with princesses, their compromises are more public so they are judged for them more than the rest of us.

On the other hand, maybe (like me) the girl always dreamed of becoming a princess. Maybe it truly is the fulfilment of her heart's desire, and she is bursting with the elation that something so improbable actually happened to her. Do we judge her for that? Do we shake our heads and pity her terrible luck and obvious gullibility, because she isn't ever going to be working at a big corporation or increasing profits for a company or doing something mundane yet "professional" because that's what modern women are supposed to want? (Keep in mind that royal families are some of the most influential conglomerates in the world; joining them is no small feat and requires no small amount of skill.)

Or maybe we should stop judging altogether.

I believe the Duchess of Cambridge is genuinely happy with her royal role. We must remember that as a smart, educated, financially secure, twenty-first-century woman, young Kate had more options for her future than any of the potential royal brides that came from generations before her. And yet *she still chose* to marry William. She still chose the life of a princess over any other career. We can't begrudge her that.

Because, at the end of the day, there is much to be said for those women who, however they reach their positions of power and privilege, *do something good with it*. After all, there are plenty of trophy wives who do nothing with their good fortune but go shopping. There are plenty of young women with trust funds who end up in rehab. Yet real princesses must have the strength of character to rise above this, to resist the temptation to use their power simply for personal gain.

Real princesses must have the foresight and courage to constantly draw the world's attention away from themselves and onto those who need it most. In fact, the sheer number of their combined charity commitments would make most of you dizzy. Queen Elizabeth II has completed more than 30,000 official engagements in her reign alone; Princess Anne is committed to no fewer than 319 charities with up to 530 engagements a year.

Some will argue that 24/7 royal "duty" combined with almost constant charity work is not healthy for women, that all women (royal or not) should stop constantly looking after others and start looking after themselves. However, I adamantly agree with Marianne Williamson when she says, "The highest form of self-care is to play it big as a citizen of the world."[11]

Real princesses not only understand this, they live it.

Below I have listed a selection of real princesses beyond Diana and Kate—those lesser-known royal women all around the world; beacons of intelligence, diplomacy, leadership, and humanitarian service; all using their regal role toward the greater good, regardless of how they obtained it.

Crown Princess Mary of Denmark

. . .

BORN: 1972, in Australia, where her father worked as a professor and her mother as a secretary. Her husband is Crown Prince Frederik, whom she met at a pub in Sydney during the 2000 Olympic Games. At the time, he simply introduced himself as "Fred."

EDUCATION: degree in commerce and law from the University of Tasmania

PREVIOUS WORK: Young & Rubicam, Microsoft

PHILANTHROPY: The Mary Foundation aims to advance cultural diversity, prevent social isolation, and encourage tolerance—with a focus on bullying and domestic violence.

MARY IS ALSO PATRON TO THE FOLLOWING:
- The Danish Refugee Council
- The Danish Youth Association of Science
- Children's Aid Foundation
- Danish Association for Mental Health
- LOKK—nationwide organization of shelters for battered women
- Maternity Worldwide
- The Danish Brain Injury Association
- The Danish Heart Association
- The Danish Kidney Association
- The Danish Mental Health Fund
- The Danish Stroke Association

Crown Princess Marie-Chantal of Greece

* * *

BORN: 1968, to an American father and a South American mother. Her husband, Crown Prince Pavlos, was the first European prince of his generation to marry a commoner, starting a trend that the princes of Norway, Spain, and Denmark soon followed.

WORK: founder and CEO of luxury children's clothing brand Marie-Chantal

PHILANTHROPY: New York School of American Ballet, Board of Venetian Heritage, London's Royal Academy, and World in Harmony—a nonprofit founded to provide humanitarian assistance to those in need (www.worldinharmony.org).

Crown Princess Masako of Japan

. . .

BORN: 1963. The daughter of a diplomat, Masako attended an American high school outside of Boston, where she obtained a 4.0 GPA and was president of the National Honor Society. "She's always had the qualities of an empress," a friend once said.[12] Her husband is Crown Prince Naruhito—although she declined his marriage proposal twice to further pursue her own career.

EDUCATION: Harvard (magna cum laude) and Oxford

LANGUAGES: (five!) English, French, German, Russian, and Japanese

PREVIOUS WORK: professional diplomat in Japan's Foreign Ministry

PHILANTHROPY: The Japanese Red Cross Society, the World Water Forum, the Asia-Pacific Water Summit

Princess Haya bint Al Hussein of Jordan

. . .

BORN: 1974. Her father is the late King Hussein I of Jordan.
PHILANTHROPY: Princess Haya founded Tkiyet Um Ali, the first Arab NGO dedicated to overcoming local hunger. She now chairs Dubai's International Humanitarian City, which is the world's largest operational center for the delivery of aid in emergencies.

Charlene, Princess of Monaco

. . .

BORN: 1978, in Rhodesia. Her husband, Prince Albert, is the son of Grace Kelly.
PREVIOUS WORK: swam in the Olympic relay team at the 2000 Sydney games
QUOTE: "I'm in a unique position where I can make a big difference. My hope is to harness the tremendous resources Monaco possesses to address a multitude of global problems."[13]
PHILANTHROPY:
- Nelson Mandela Day
- The World Wildlife Fund
- The Princess Grace Foundation
- The Monaco Red Cross
- The Born Free Foundation
- Fight Aids Monaco

Princess Angela of Liechtenstein

• • •

BORN: 1958. Her husband is Prince Maximilian of Liechtenstein.

EDUCATION/ WORK: A standout graduate of the Parsons School of Design in New York, Angela worked as a fashion director for Adrienne Vittadini. She is currently the only princess of African American decent within a reigning European dynasty.

Princess Claire of Luxembourg

• • •

BORN: 1985, in Germany. Her husband is Prince Félix of Luxembourg.

LANGUAGES: German, English, French, Italian

WORK HISTORY: Condé Nast, UNESCO Department of Bioethics and Human Rights

EDUCATION: BA in international communication from the American University in Paris; master's degree in bioethics from Pontifical Athenaeum Regina Apostolorum in Rome, graduating summa cum laude; and a visiting scholar at the Kennedy Institute of Ethics at Georgetown University, Washington, DC. She is currently pursuing a doctorate in the ethics of organ donation.

Princess Laurentien of the Netherlands

. . .

BORN: 1966. Her husband is Prince Constantijn, son of Queen Beatrix and Prince Claus.
PHILANTHROPY: UNESCO special envoy on literacy for development and corecipient of the Major Bosshardt Prize for her work in combating illiteracy.

Crown Princess Mette-Marit of Norway

. . .

BORN: 1973. Mette-Marit already had a three-year-old son (out of wedlock) when she met Crown Prince Haakon at a rock concert, but he didn't think twice about her less-than-conventional past. Totally smitten, the prince shocked the world by welcoming Mette-Marit and her son into his home, and within months he proposed to her—shattering royal stereotypes about what a "proper" princess should be.
PHILANTHROPY: Forum for Women and Development, the Norwegian Red Cross, the Norwegian Council for Mental Health
FUTURE GIRL POWER: Her daughter, Ingrid, is the Hereditary Princess of Norway.

Princess Madeleine of Sweden

. . .

BORN: 1982. Her parents are King Carl XVI Gustaf and Queen Silvia of Sweden.

EDUCATION: BA in art, ethnology, and modern history from Stockholm University

QUOTE: "At one point in my life I said to myself, I'm a princess—so what should I do? To just cut ribbons is not enough for me. I want to make a greater contribution. I believe that if everyone helped just a little, the world would be a better place. Not everyone needs to move mountains, but we can all pick up a piece of sand."[14]

PHILANTHROPY: UNICEF, the World Childhood Foundation

Crown Princess Victoria of Sweden

. . .

BORN: 1977. Her parents are King Carl XVI Gustaf and Queen Silvia of Sweden. She became Crown Princess in 1980, when Sweden became the first country to adopt absolute primogeniture (meaning no preference is paid to either gender when determining the order of precedence for the throne).

EDUCATION: Political science and history at Yale University, conflict resolution at Uppsala University, the Swedish National Defense College, the Ministry for Foreign Affairs' Diplomat Program

INTERNSHIPS: United Nations in New York, Swedish Embassy in Washington, DC

LANGUAGES: English, French, German, Swedish

PHILANTHROPY: The Crown Princess Victoria Fund and the Swedish International Development Cooperation Agency

FUTURE GIRL POWER: Her daughter Estelle is the Hereditary Princess of Sweden.

Princess Maha Chakri Sirindhorn of Thailand

. . .

BORN: 1955. Her father is King Bhumibol Adulyadej. In Thailand, she is known as the "Princess of Technology" due to her interest and expertise in applying science for the country's development.

EDUCATION: holds a degree in history and a doctorate in educational development

LANGUAGES: English, French, Chinese

WORK: head of the History Department at the Chulachomklao Royal Military Academy

Princess Bajrakitiyabha of Thailand

. . .

BORN: 1978. Her parents are Crown Prince Maha Vajiralongkorn and Princess Soamsavali.

EDUCATION: Cornell Law School

WORK: UN Women goodwill ambassador; attorney for the Office of the Attorney General in Bangkok; currently Thailand's ambassador to Austria

PHILANTHROPY: The princess founded the Kamlangjai project to support Thai women in incarceration, including pregnant inmates and their babies. She also sponsors a foundation to help rural areas affected by natural disasters.

Princess Anne
(of the United Kingdom and Commonwealth realms)

. . .

BORN: 1950. She is Queen Elizabeth II's only daughter.

PHILANTHROPY: Often described as "the best king the country never had," Princess Anne is associated with no fewer than 319 charity organizations and often carries out up to 530 engagements a year. Those she is most closely involved with include:

- The Save the Children Fund; Anne has been president since 1970 (www.savethechildren.org.uk).
- The Princess Royal Trust for Carers (www.carers.org)

Princess Beatrice of York
(of the United Kingdom and Commonwealth realms)

. . .

BORN: 1988. Her parents are Prince Andrew and Sarah, Duchess of York. Her grandmother is Queen Elizabeth II. After Princess Charlotte, Beatrice is the first female in the line of succession to the throne of the UK and fifteen other Commonwealth realms.

EDUCATION: history degree from Goldsmiths University

INTERNSHIP: UK Foreign and Commonwealth Office

WORK: Sony Pictures

PHILANTHROPY:

- Children in Crisis. Beatrice was their first ever junior ambassador. She recently auctioned the infamous hat she wore to Will and Kate's wedding, donating all proceeds to the charity (www.childrenincrisis.org).
- The Teenage Cancer Trust (www.teenagecancertrust.org)
- The Big Change Charitable Trust. Founded by Beatrice and six friends, the charity supports projects to improve the lives of young people (www.bigchangecharitabletrust.org).
- Also patron to the Helen Arkell Dyslexia Centre, the Sick Kids Friends Foundation, the Forget Me Not Children's Hospice and the Broomwood African Education Foundation

Princess Eugenie of York
(of the United Kingdom and Commonwealth realms)

. . .

BORN: 1990. Her parents are Prince Andrew and Sarah, Duchess of York. Her grandmother is Queen Elizabeth II.

EDUCATION: Having studied English and history of art at Newcastle University, she is one of the brightest members of the Windsor family, with A-level exam results that broke all royal records.

WORK EXPERIENCE: Christie's auction house; Paddle8

PHILANTHROPY:

- Kids Company (www.kidsco.org.uk)
- Children in Crisis (www.childrenincrisis.org)
- Elephant Family (www.elephantfamily.org)

PASSIVE? BRAINLESS? SUPERFICIAL?

I don't think so.

Chapter VII

IN DEFENSE OF
THE PRINCE

. . . . .

*The most important career decision you're
going to make is whether or not you have a
life partner and who that partner is.*

– SHERYL SANDBERG, COO OF FACEBOOK
AND AUTHOR OF *LEAN IN*

*Pursue all of your dreams. Not just the
ones that are politically popular.*

– SUSAN PATTON, AUTHOR OF *MARRY SMART*

W E ARE NOT SUPPOSED to want to fall in love with a
prince. No way. Not if we are intelligent women with
any sense of self. And we're *definitely* not supposed
to believe in the old-fashioned fairy tale of true love. Forget that.
It's much more acceptable for modern, educated women to pretend
that our dreams of happily ever after don't exist. But I'm afraid that
doesn't make them go away.

When the princess dream is attacked, when fairytale narratives are attacked, there are several issues that seem to cause unease: Do we really want our daughters to think that a mythical prince can save them? Do we really want girls to focus on snaring wealthy husbands instead of their own careers? And do we really want girls to think that marriage is the ultimate goal in life?

Of course the answer to all of the above is no.

But these questions miss the point.

The princess dream is not about rescue. Or social climbing. Or gold digging.

It's about knowing that no matter what your circumstances, you are *worthy of a prince.* He may be rich, he may be poor; you might marry him, you might not—but he sees you, and loves you, for the princess that you are. And you are allowed to love him back.

I HARDLY NEED TO tell you that in 1979, my hippie parents gave me the *Free to Be . . . You and Me* record album. And I listened to it occasionally, whenever I grew tired of my *Snow White* record. Produced by Marlo Thomas, the album had a bright pink cover (to which no one objected), kid-friendly lyrics, and stories filled with "progressive" 1970s ideas: boys can play with dolls, mommies can have careers, and children can grow up to be whatever they want to be.

But the story on that record that I remember the most was that of Atalanta—a princess from Greek mythology "who runs like the wind" and who isn't interested in marrying anytime soon. (Disney's Merida in *Brave* comes to mind here.)

Here's the story: Atalanta's father, the King, invites all the princes in the land to compete in a race; the winner of which gets to marry his daughter. Atalanta agrees to this but only if she can enter the race herself and choose her own husband (or none at all) if she wins. Doubtful she will run faster than the men, the King agrees to his daughter's terms and allows her to run in the race.

Needless to say, Atalanta "runs like the wind," but one prince catches up to her and begins running "side by side with her, as her equal"—and they end up winning the race together.

The King tries to name this prince as the victor and offers Atalanta to him as his prize. But the (rather liberal-minded) prince won't marry Atalanta unless *she also wants to marry him*. In the end, they become good friends, decide that maybe they'll marry someday, and, in the meantime, Atalanta goes off to explore the world.

During my personal quest for Prince Charming (whether he was real or metaphorical), this story has always been in the background. I saw no reason why I couldn't chose my own prince instead of waiting for him to come to me. And I saw no reason why we couldn't go through life "side by side, as equals." But the fact that I wanted him to *be* "a prince" was nonnegotiable.

It is so often misunderstood, but the truth of the matter is this: when little girls set their sights on finding "a prince" (real or conceptual), they are actually making a very strong statement about *their own self-worth*.

It boils down to a simple Jungian impulse, says Lisa Phillips in her wonderful book *Unrequited*: "I want this person because I want to be like him."[1]

In her book *Committed*, Elizabeth Gilbert further explains that we choose partners to express the deepest aspirations that we have for ourselves: "your spouse becomes the most gleaming possible mirror through which your emotional individualism is reflected back to the world."[2]

Wanting to marry "Prince Charming" simply means that young girls are in touch with their inner highness in a way that grown-ups are not. They are born understanding that they are worthy of nothing but the best and see no reason why they shouldn't aim for the stars. It is only when adults start telling them that princes only exist in fairy tales that they begin to accept that maybe they should settle for less than exceptional.

If a twenty-year-old girl confided to you, "My boyfriend is not really what I'm looking for but I don't think I can do any better,"—would you let her get away with thinking that? Of course not. So why is it acceptable to tell six-year-old girls that princes are imaginary and that settling for less is the only way forward?

I would hope it goes without saying that women of all ages must embrace the fundamental truth that personal fulfillment cannot be found through the perfect man. But think how many unhealthy relationships could be prevented if, rather than telling our girls that princes aren't real, we told them not to stop looking until Prince Charming was standing right in front of them.

If this was the status quo, if "Prince Charming" was the *minimum* standard women would accept—maybe men would up their game. And maybe things like chivalry, courtesy, gallantry, and valor would become givens—not optional extras.

IS A LITTLE ROMANCE REALLY SO BAD?

. . .

The root of the word courage is cor—
the Latin word for heart.

WHEN TALKING TO PARENTS about fairy tales and Disney movies, what I found interesting is that most of them didn't really object to the scary plot lines involving dead parents and evil curses. Instead, if parents objected to anything it was how the fairytale narratives put too much emphasis on romantic love. (Because we all know there is nothing scarier than that!) They told me they opposed the "unrealistic" endings which usually involved a married couple, deeply in love and running off to a castle in the sunset.

At this point, I always reminded them that the Grimms' descriptions of royal weddings were hardly blissful affairs of sweetness and light. Go back and read them—it's really rather disturbing: Cinderella's stepsisters are her bridesmaids but have their eyes pecked out by birds after the ceremony; Snow White's stepmother attends the wedding of the princess she tried to kill but is forced to dance the night away in shoes filled with white hot coals until she dies. (Yes, it's grotesque, but children respond to it; they are comforted by the fact that evil is punished.)

We also must look at historical context. For centuries, women were the primary tellers of fairytales, and, for them, a marriage of companionship involving the right to choose one's spouse on the basis of love—rather than economic or political advantage—was actually a very progressive objective.

Bruno Bettelheim will tell you that fairytale stories are not really about romantic love at all but about helping children learn autonomy and to deal with the anxiety of one day separating from their parents. As many children today don't grow up with the security of a well-integrated community, this is a comforting message to take away.

And lately even Disney has slowly veered away from the traditional happily-ever-after script. In 2007, *Enchanted*'s Princess Giselle and Prince Edward didn't love each other at all, and in 2012 *Brave*'s Princess Merida had no interest in finding love whatsoever. *Frozen* (2013) warns about the dangers of love at first sight (which, incidentally, I find totally unnecessary since happiness can be, and often is, found this way) and shows how family love can be just as powerful as romantic love.

That same year, *Maleficent* made a great case against falling for any guy who might one day inhabit a throne. Based on *Sleeping Beauty*, the movie turns the well-known fairy tale into one of redemption rather than romance, as we watch Maleficent learn that the truest love comes not from any man but from within oneself (a transformational theme that underlies all the original fairy tales if we are wise enough to see it).

But, when it comes to fairytale romance, I guess the question parents really want to ask me is this: Is it possible for a girl (be she real or imaginary) to fall in love with "a prince" *and* still be a strong woman?

I always shake my head at the absurdity of this.

Yes, being a princess means following your heart, but by no means has it ever implied that you must leave your brain, your confidence, or your self-worth behind.

And even so, there's a lot to be said for the heart!

The power of love is so easily discounted, so easily dismissed.

Yet in *Frozen*, love thaws an entire kingdom. In *Snow White*, *Sleeping Beauty*, *The Little Mermaid*, and *Beauty and the Beast*, curse after curse after curse is broken by love.

Perhaps all of us should take it more seriously.

DARING TO DREAM

. . .

WHEN I WAS A teenager, everyone thought I was crazy (more than crazy—*delusional*) for wanting to marry an English prince. They called me silly, shallow, and superficial. But, more than that, they called me arrogant for daring to dream so high above my station.

Dreaming.

Setting high standards.

That's what *really* upsets people.

Even girls like Kate Middleton aren't above censure if princes are involved. When Kate finally got engaged to Prince William, most of England was overjoyed. But I also heard plenty of snarky whispers, all akin to this: "isn't Kate clever in hooking herself such a husband?"—as if she tricked or bewitched him into marrying her.

When Charlene Wittstock became engaged to Prince Albert of Monaco, everyone was certain she must be after his fortune; after all "she couldn't possibly be with him for his looks." (It never occurred to anyone she might be with him for love.)

And what about men who marry into royal families? Why does no one ever mention them? Why does no one accuse *them* of social climbing or gold digging?

Most men who marry into royal families know full well that they can't pass on their surnames to their children and instead will be enveloped by the wife's royal house. But not a peep from the gender police.

HRH Prince Philip (the Queen's husband) knew when he married the young Princess Elizabeth in 1947 that after her coronation he would be required to walk *two paces behind her* forevermore. Daniel Westling was Victoria of Sweden's personal trainer before he became her prince consort, yet there was no critical uproar questioning his motives. Same for Princess Märtha Louise of Norway, who married an author, and Princess Alexia of Greece, who married a sailor. Why is it that, when men marry princesses, it must be for love, yet, when women marry princes, it is thought that surely there must be a darker, more selfish objective? So much for gender equality.

LOVE DOESN'T MAKE YOU WEAK

. . .

Yes! I think it's possible to be a feminist and be in love!

— LENA DUNHAM

A WOMAN SHOULD NEVER be criticized for falling in love.

I actually know several women who have turned away from the very idea of feminism precisely because they think today's feminism doesn't allow for true love. And I understand where they're coming from; I almost went down that path myself. (A handsome prince vs. boring feminism? If I had to choose, it wasn't a contest.)

But women will always feel trapped if we continue to think we must choose between using our heads and using our hearts.

I understand that instead of wanting "a prince," society tells you you're supposed to want to be an attorney or a genetics professor or a NASA scientist. But who says you can't marry "a prince" *and* become a Supreme Court justice? Who says you can't find true love and find the cure for cancer? And who says you can't have a fairy-tale wedding and pilot the first mission to Mars?

Not me.

Did Oprah have to choose between the love of her life and her media empire? Did the Queen of England have to choose between her kingdom and Prince Philip? Did Margaret Thatcher have to choose between her husband and the office of prime minster? Did Nancy Pelosi have to choose between her marriage and becoming the highest-ranking female politician in American history? Of course not. But if they listened to some of these fairytale naysayers, they might have.

The desire for romantic love doesn't make women weak—it makes us human. And I'm certain if you probed deep into the hearts of the fiercest fairytale critics, beneath all the bravado, you'd find the tender souls of traditionalists. Because, deep down, every little girl dreams of finding her Prince Charming—not just every little girl but every young woman, every old woman, in every country, in every century. It doesn't matter if it's Cleopatra or Kate Middleton, Elizabeth Bennet or Carrie Bradshaw, Lady Diana or Lady Gaga. Deep down, while we may not wish literally for a prince and a castle, we do wish for them figuratively. We all want a guy who acts like a prince, and we all want a home that feels like our castle.

And, just as women should never be criticized for falling in love, they should never be criticized if they happen to "marry well." In no way am I saying that women should attach themselves and their livelihood to wealthy or powerful men without some sort of a safety net. But we have to acknowledge that successful men are attractive for many legitimate reasons and women shouldn't be punished for that. Nor should women be made to feel less worthy because they come from a lower socioeconomic background than the man in their lives or because they don't hold an equivalent job title or earn the same amount as he does. *All women* bring untold value to their relationships. It's not always compensated for fairly or in traditional monetary terms, but it's value nonetheless. And to suggest anything else is really quite demeaning.

And is wanting a fairytale marriage really such a terrible thing? We all know that modern women don't really *need* marriage. We can have sex without marriage, children without marriage, money and status without marriage. If we're honest with ourselves, we know that there are few logical reasons for any woman to rush to the altar, much less with the giant dress, the giant cake, all the stress, expense, and fairytale-style pomp and circumstance of Cinderella or Kate Middleton.

And yet we do.

So does that mean all the intelligent, independent, well-educated women that I know are simply being hoodwinked by Disney? Bamboozled by the wedding industry? Or is there more to it than that?

Feminist author Naomi Wolf says that there is. And here is where it gets really interesting.

Wolf declares that modern weddings, with all their silly trappings, allow women's *"repressed regal nature to emerge . . .* with the sparkling tiara, sweeping train, and attendants; with the great 'aura' cast by the veil; the suitor offering gems on bended knee, and the great moment when the entire court turns to watch her make her awe-inspiring entrance. . . . All this gives women back, for a day, the buried psychological dimension in which *they know they are rulers by nature."*[3]

It's no wonder we're so obsessed with fairytale weddings.

It's because our inner princess is desperate to be recognized.

Desperate to begin her reign.

PRINCELY APPEAL

• • •

MY FIRST LITERARY AGENT took me on as a client purely because she used to have a childhood crush on Prince Edward (the Queen's youngest son) and she related so much to my own childhood quest for royal romance. This agent promptly sent my manuscript to a New York editor who used to have a childhood crush on Prince Albert of Monaco. And just like that, it all came together in a perfect storm of princely crushes, and, quite suddenly, I had a book deal. The commercial thinking was that if the three of us (three educated, intelligent, professional women) could all have had crushes on a prince—then surely other women out there did to. We were right. Nearly ten years later, women still contact me to divulge their secret feelings for various royal heartthrobs from monarchies all over the world.

And this phenomenon is not just confined to dreamy middle-aged women; passion for princes seems to carry on into each subsequent generation.

Back in the days when his cheeks had color and his head had hair, Prince William was indisputably the world's favorite royal pinup. In fact, the moment Buckingham Palace announced that William would be attending Scotland's St. Andrews University, applications from American girls skyrocketed. (And I'm not surprised. If I'd been just five years younger, I would've applied in a heartbeat.) Because of Prince William, there are now five times as many American students at St. Andrews, representing more than 20 percent of the school's entire population! Hence, the star power of an eligible prince.

But, sadly, in November 2010, that glorious eligibility came to end (and, sadly, so did much of William's hair). At the time, I remember receiving an invite to join a worldwide Facebook group called "A little part of me died when Prince William got engaged." Another friend promptly sent me an (unofficial) commemorative royal wedding souvenir: a real china plate embossed with the royal wedding date and the words "It should have been me." I laughed, but also marveled at the fact that there was clearly a market for such an item.

With William officially off the shelf, for a week or two, it seemed as if the entire female population was in some kind of mourning. But it couldn't last forever because everyone couldn't help but adore William's luminous bride-to-be.

And then, before anyone knew what was happening, Prince Harry, with his freckly face and fiery hair, suddenly emerged as the hottest prince in the land. (Here's to you, Harry. I didn't see it coming.)

William has a huge sense of duty, but it's Harry who has the laidback magnetism and the sexy, mischievous grin. Watching Harry in action, it's hard not to think of his legendary mother. Harry's clearly inherited Diana's natural empathy, allowing him to connect easily with people from all walks of life. In fact, Harry has often declared his determination to honor his mother's memory by further embracing her charity work: "I want to carry on the things she didn't quite finish," he says.

It's no wonder legions of girls around the world are going weak at the knees.

When I was interviewed by *Newsweek* about Kate and William's upcoming wedding, I mentioned in passing to the reporter how many letters I get from girls confessing their love for Prince Harry (and it's true: I get hundreds of letters). Before I knew what was happening, the prewedding story had turned into "Invasion of the Harry Hunters," and "Harry hunting" had somehow become my new specialty subject on an international scale. TV producers began contacting me in droves, wanting my help to televise the concept (but they were quickly derailed by a terrible reality show called *I Wanna Marry Harry*).

Despite the media circus that tries to capitalize on Harry's allure, the timeless theme remains the same: girls go gaga for princes.

Always have, always will.

NOT ENOUGH PRINCE

. . .

ACTRESS EMMA WATSON, THE new "it girl" of feminism thanks to her incredible UN speech, was recently rumored to be romantically linked to Prince Harry. She denied the rumors via Twitter but added this: "marrying a Prince is not a prerequisite for being a Princess."

If only all women understood this.

Meanwhile, Prince Harry made headlines around the world when compromising photographs of his Las Vegas hijinks were published. If I remember correctly, a game of "strip billiards" was involved. Part of me laughed, part of me was horrified—and that charming contradiction is precisely why Harry remains the media's darling.

Looking back on the incident two years later, Harry remarked, "It was just a classic case of me being too much army and not enough prince."[4]

Harry is not known for his intellect, but I was struck by the wisdom of those words: *not enough prince.*

Imagine if that phrase became part of the popular vernacular when dealing with young boys, and when dealing with young men in general. Imagine if all dishonorable male behavior could be viciously labelled as "not enough prince." Imagine if boys seriously took that sentiment to heart and became genuinely disappointed in themselves for not living up to this princely ideal. Maybe things would start changing. Maybe men would start realizing that codes of chivalry don't just belong in Arthurian legend but create the foundation for respectful and compassionate behavior in this day and age as well. Maybe men would understand that real courage and real honor is not only refusing to demean women but speaking up when others do. Maybe one in three women would no longer be raped or beaten.

Maybe instead of telling our girls that their brains are filled with too much princess, we should focus on telling our boys that *their* brains don't contain nearly enough prince.

Chapter VIII

IN DEFENSE OF FEMININE POWER (YOUR INNER PRINCESS)

· · · · ·

*The purpose of life as a woman is to ascend
her throne and rule with the heart.*

– MARIANNE WILLIAMSON

Women who seek to be equal with men lack ambition.

– TIMOTHY LEARY

A FEW YEARS AGO (AFTER I realized that becoming a published author wouldn't allow me to immediately retire), I came up with a quirky business idea. I knew I loved princesses and I knew I loved royal history, and I thought it would be fun to create an educational program for girls that incorporated both. So Princess Prep was born.

The idea was to offer a week in London for little girls (ages seven to ten) to explore real castles while learning about royal history, royal etiquette, and the positive attributes of both real and fictional princesses. I wanted it to be an alternative Bibbity Bobbity Boutique—something that would inspire girls to think more deeply about what it means to be a princess.

I also wanted it to be a fun experience, something that I would have loved at that age—so I filled the prospective itinerary with afternoon tea, a pony ride through Hyde Park, a day of "princess volunteer work," and a night at the theater. I designed and built the website completely by myself and took out a tiny, yet hugely expensive, ad in the *New York Times* summer camp section.

There were tons of "luxury" camps out there at the time catering to all kinds of hobbies: polo camps in Argentina, surfing camps in Hawaii, ice climbing camps in the Alps, and so on. I figured there had to be room in the market for *my* idea. Personally, I never liked the super-outdoorsy options available when I was a child and would have killed to have an excuse to go to England for a week.

So the ad came out. And at first there was radio silence.

But then, as if I had planned it, Prince William's engagement to Kate Middleton was announced. And overnight I couldn't keep up with the press requests. The global media were obsessed with my idea, and interest in Princes Prep skyrocketed. In the midst of the chaos, I did my best to be a savvy businesswoman even though I really had no idea what I was doing. Hoping to capitalize on the world's newfound fascination with all things regal and British, I quickly organized a series of "royal tea parties" for little girls to celebrate the upcoming royal wedding.

These were simple and quite silly afternoons where we learned to curtsey (to a cardboard cutout of the Queen) and how to formally address William and Kate (Your Royal Highness, in case you're wondering). For fun we practiced walking with books on our heads and finished with tea and scones.

London's American expats clamored to these parties en masse. And so did the world's press. I was shocked at the coverage these modest events were receiving—from the *Guardian* to the *Boston Globe* to the *LA Times* to *Time* magazine to BBC World, CNN, ABC, CBS, NBC, and every European news agency you can think of. Each time, I literally had to turn away dozens of cameras at the door.

I wasn't complaining, but what was the big deal? Had no one ever seen a tea set before? Was I the only person on the planet who knew how to curtsey? I was baffled.

But I became even more baffled as time went on.

The first thing that surprised me was that, when mothers contacted me about possibly enrolling their daughters in the camp, almost without exception, they would ask whether something similar existed for grown women. From South America to China to Chicago, these grown-up ladies weren't just interested in afternoon tea—they wanted the full royal tour and the full princess education that came with it. I was unprepared to deal with this demand and hardly ready to start an international travel company. But yet again I was seeing just how deeply the princess archetype was embedded in women's hearts (adult hearts!) around the world.

I did some fast research on the "adult princess market" and discovered that the grown-up princess dream brings more than 36,000 grown women to Disney World every year to run the Disney Princess Half Marathon—all while wearing tiaras and dressed as their favorite princess character. I also learned that Walt Disney World has hosted more than 30,000 grown-up weddings and offers an elaborate princess collection of wedding gowns (each style named after a different royal heroine). Combined with the reaction to my memoir and the crazy reaction to my camp, none of this really surprised me. After all, I knew better than anyone that you simply don't "outgrow" a princess dream.

Later that month, nearly 2 billion people (*a third of the planet!*) watched Catherine Middleton walk down the aisle of Westminster Abbey and become a princess. After reading that statistic, I knew it was no longer just a hunch of mine; it was now overwhelmingly clear: women around the world (*billions* of women!) were desperate to connect with their inner princess.

Meanwhile, the more press coverage my princess events received, the more I was attacked. Apparently some journalists thought the very idea of my princess camp was setting the feminist movement back hundreds of years. When I received a request to appear on a popular television talk show as the "antifeminist" voice, I'd had enough.

Was it so impossible, *so unthinkable* for a woman to be pro-princess *and* profeminist?

Not if I have anything to do with it.

RECLAIMING OUR LOST PRINCESS

*   *   *

Telling women their innate glory is their biggest weakness is the oldest trick in the patriarchal book.

– MARIANNE WILLIAMSON

THE PRINCESS DREAM SHOULD never be insulted. And certainly not in the name of feminism.

I'm a feminist. This means I have basic rights to life, liberty, and happiness; I want to vote, not be owned by my husband, get paid fairly for my work, have control over my body, have the same opportunities as men, and not ever be raped or beaten. (Come to think of it, being a feminist is not really a political viewpoint—it's just true.)

Feminism is about the freedom to be anything we want; it's about expanding our choices, not constraining them. And, that said, I have zero patience for women who tell other women what they can and cannot do, what they can and cannot be, and what they can and cannot dream about.

We can't go around saying that modern feminism means we can be *anything*—and then five seconds later say, "Oh, *except* you can't be a princess."

It's ridiculous. When women stoop to the level of policing their own gender, I see little to distinguish them from the sexist forces they claim to be fighting against.

It's not that I don't respect feminist movements of the past. Because I do. Reverently. Susan B. Anthony and I went to the same college (my dorm was named after her!), and it has hardly escaped my attention that, because of her efforts, I am able to vote.

And before my mom and her hippie friends came along, I know women faced sexism of a kind that I can only vaguely imagine when I watch *Mad Men*. (As my mom likes to remind me, I probably wouldn't be able to wear jeans or go on the pill if it weren't for their efforts.) There's no denying that all women have reaped untold benefits thanks to feminists of the past, and I'm tremendously grateful to them.

But studies show that although women as a whole have made substantial gains, the "equality" my mother's wave of feminism set out to achieve has not happened, and we are even less happy today than our predecessors were in 1972.[1]

The question is, why? There are two simple reasons. The first is that too many women have been fighting for the wrong kind of equality—the kind that requires a woman to act like a man in a man's world. The second reason is that *true equality*—the kind that allows men and women to celebrate their differences and embrace a healthy yin and yang of symbiotic power—is continually stifled. Somewhere along the way, old-school feminism made an unforgivable error: to belittle all things feminine in the name of feminism. And the princess genre is just one of many "feminine" things that is constantly belittled.

Think about it. We hate ourselves for buying Diana biographies. We lie about watching news that involves Kate Middleton. We are skeptical of letting our daughters have princess-themed birthday parties. And so on and so on. But it doesn't stop there. We are also careful to suppress our feminine strengths at every single board meeting. We are afraid to be too empathetic, too diplomatic, too collaborative. We are afraid to show emotion. We are afraid to be kind. It's not only absurd—it's outrageous. As women, our collective inner princess has not only been silenced, she has been invalidated.

But the recent and increasing obsession with princesses by young girls and women of all ages is overwhelming proof that we *have had enough*. We want our feminine power back.

Through whatever means necessary, we are ready to reclaim our inner princess. And she is not helpless, passive, and frivolous—she is strong, she is brave, she is daring, and she is powerful.

PUTTING THE FEMININE
BACK INTO FEMINISM

. . .

Tenderness and kindness are not signs of weakness,
but manifestations of strength and resolution.

– KAHLIL GIBRAN

WHEN IT COMES TO nature versus nurture, the scientific jury is still out (and may be out for quite some time). But the truth is, regardless of the gender we are assigned at birth or how we are raised, most of us gravitate toward behaviors that are deemed feminine or masculine (or a mix of both).

Most of us would agree that dismissing someone purely because she is female is unacceptable. Yet dismissing feminine qualities and feminine expression (including princess culture) is still widely condoned.

But it has to stop. Because the feminism of the future won't be about how to succeed in the masculine world but how to empower the feminine world. We don't need to figure out how to make women stronger; women are *already* strong. What we need to do is start changing how that strength is viewed.

Most women I know are deeply unfulfilled precisely because they are constantly suppressing their feminine strengths; searching in vain for power and happiness within the confines of the patriarchal world. According to the book *Gender Intelligence*, women are continually encouraged to "take charge of their careers as men would—no matter how inauthentic or uninviting it feels." [2]

"Leaning in" is certainly an option. But not if the result supports the same masculine system that makes women so miserable.

Sometimes I feel princess detractors are actually saying this: "You can't like princesses. They reflect a value system that I don't respect. Why don't you create a life where you sit in an alpha-male office environment for ten hours a day, and force yourself to adapt to their male-defined corporate culture instead?"

Right now, the status quo is not a value system I respect. And there is no point in killing ourselves to reach the top of the ladder if we already know it's leaning against the wrong wall.

Perhaps we should stop talking so much about getting women to "lean in" to masculine jobs and focus more on getting men to "lean out" into feminine ones. Because true gender equality is about valuing *everyone's* work—the caregivers as well as the breadwinners. It's about using terms like "working father" just as often as we say "working mother." It's about stopping to question why we continue to devalue anyone the minute they care for others or show the smallest sign of nurturing or maternal (read: feminine) behavior.

"Women will continue to be oppressed, politically and socially," warns Marianne Williamson, "until we recognise that the roles traditionally associated with women are among the most important in our society." [3]

Feminine skills are not inferior skills; they are *essential* skills. And, as queens in the making, it is imperative that we reclaim them as our own.

In the meantime, we must stop accepting male behavior and male choices as the default ideal. Because if women continue to measure themselves by the standards of a male-defined culture, by comparison we will always seem deficient.

Polly Vernon, author of *Hot Feminist*, brilliantly describes this dilemma:

> I am bored by the notion that male behavioral patterns are the gold standard of all available behavioral patterns. By the notion that if women ever hope to get anywhere at all, we need to start being more like Them, and less like Us. . . . That we need to shout down the competition like a man, 'lean in' like a man; brag about our achievements, and screw over whoever gets in our way, because that's the only sort of behavior men understand. . . . Well, maybe it is; but every time we tell women that the things we do—by instinct, conditioning, or habit—are not adequate or powerful and that we should override them in favour of the base notion that the male way equals the right way, we do all women an injustice.[4]

You see, the trouble didn't begin with glass ceilings in the workplace or unrealistic photographs in fashion magazines. And it certainly didn't begin with pink toys or Disney princess movies. The trouble began much earlier, when women became convinced by whomever or whatever that *the girl* within them was not good enough.

Women should be honoring the feminine wisdom inherent in our true selves and listening to our inner voice—yet, from girlhood on, there are endless forces trying to get us to take off our plastic tiaras and do exactly the opposite. In the end, little girls grow into women who do not value themselves as women, who deny the power of their femininity, and who constantly silence the call of their inner princess.

But, observes Naomi Wolf, "reawakening in the female psyche are new incarnations of female power that have long been foreshadowed in the old archetypes."[5]

This is why, despite all the critics, the princess genre is growing at lightning speed—today's girls are drawn to it naturally, but grown-up girls perpetuate it (some secretly, some not so secretly) because they are *desperate* for it. Everyone is desperate to reconnect with our lost feminine power.

When I say feminine power, I'm not taking about darning socks or cooking the perfect pot roast. I'm taking about nonviolence, diplomatic communication, compassionate leadership, looking after those less fortunate, and caring for those not able to care for themselves. Feminine power is emotional intelligence, intuitive knowing, and the ability to see the holistic nature of problems and solutions.

(And I'm not saying women are the only ones who can embrace this type of thinking; some of the best men in the world already have. Think Gandhi. Think Martin Luther King Jr.)

"Power doesn't have to be fierce," says Elizabeth Gilbert, author of *Eat, Pray, Love*. "It doesn't have to be aggressive or combative. It doesn't have to be in your face. True power has nothing to do with status, nothing to do with reputation, and nothing to do with winning. Because you can achieve all that stuff (status, reputation, victory) and still feel lost as hell."[6]

And we do feel lost as hell. Power that comes from an external source is false and fleeting, yet *true* power—the kind that comes from within—is authentic and enduring. Most women are not experiencing their true power because they are afraid to embrace their feminine strengths.

"It's time to acknowledge that scapegoating femininity is the Achilles' heel of the feminist movement," declares *Ms. Magazine* blogger Julia Serano. "While past feminists have gone to great lengths to tear away the negative connotations that plagued women's bodies and biology, they've allowed the negative connotations associated with femininity to persist unabated. . . . Most reasonable people see women and men as equals, but few (if any) dare to claim that femininity is masculinity's equal."[7]

Well, I'm claiming it. And, consciously or not, everyone who likes princesses is claiming it too. It's high time we start putting the feminine back into feminism.

Because nobody is going to listen to us until we start listening to ourselves.

IN DEFENSE OF
NATURAL FEMALE STRENGTHS

. . .

We can manage to be more than the body,
but there is no way we can be less.

– JOAN GOULD

AT OUR VERY CORE, women are life-bringers, nurturers, healers. Women, like princesses, lead by example—not by force—and do so with grace and compassion. We possess a fierce and quite powerful urge to protect our nest, protect our planet, and protect all living things upon it. Of course we can do absolutely anything else that we put our minds to, but, to fully reconnect with our inner princess, we must stop ignoring the skills at which we naturally excel.

I find it ironic that those who hate princess culture often believe they are promoting female diversity when in reality it seems they want everyone to be exactly the same: genderless. Yet we are not born androgynous; *there are* inherent differences between boys and girls that are not programmed by society. In no way do these differences mean that it's pointless to strive for equality, but we must acknowledge that biology matters. Equal in value is not the same as identical.

We can't escape the fact that women have ovaries, wombs, and breasts, a biological reality that tends to seriously and inevitably affect the course of our lives. It has nothing to do with stereotyping and everything to do with basic proliferation of the species.

Evolution has programmed women to reproduce, to nurture rather than fight, to love rather than destroy. Women are better at reading body language and nonverbal cues; we have greater emotional sensitivity; stronger empathy; better senses of touch, taste, and smell; more patience; an excellent ability to multitask; a penchant for long-term planning; a flair for networking and negotiating; and a strong preference for cooperating and reaching consensus. As a result, girls play differently, fight differently, learn differently, process emotions differently, and experience the world differently than boys do.

I know it's popular to believe that gender differences would vanish if we raised girls to play with trucks and encouraged boys to play with dolls. Or that gender equality would prevail if we cuddled and coddled the boys more often while we played more "rough and tumble" games with the girls. Yet no scientific evidence exists that supports the claim that gender-neutral child rearing has any measurable benefit.[8]

Of course none of us are completely bound to our biological predispositions, but ignoring reasonable observations about how the sexes differ does nothing to further the feminist cause.

"If anything, feminism should be a celebration of our own unique characteristics," declares author Marianne Williamson, "not an assertion that women have no unique characteristics."[9]

There's an onslaught of research showing that gender differences in brain functioning and behavior are *not* simply the result of social forces—but for whatever reason, this research is continuously ignored. And in the grown-up world, this means female strengths are not recognized, not valued, and not maximized.

To systemically ignore female strengths is not progressive or unbiased—it's crazy. Because treating women exactly like men doesn't help them—it holds them back.

I concede that being treated exactly like men is definitely better than being treated worse than men. But we're beyond that now. And for everyone's sake, we must move forward. Especially when the research is so compelling.

It is scientifically proven that women have better hearing than men—which means they are more effective listeners, and more able to inspire trust.[10] *It is scientifically proven* that women are better at interpreting facial expressions than men (whereas men boast excellent focus when it comes to moving objects)—which means women are better at detecting emotional nuances in social situations.[11] *It is scientifically proven* that estrogen multiplies linguistic pathways, enhancing both verbal memory and articulation, allowing women to communicate more effectively than men.[12]

It doesn't stop there. *It is scientifically proven* that women define power differently—preferring to create cooperative connections rather than pursue a higher rank (yet for men it is the reverse).[13] *It is scientifically proven* that women prefer collaborative, consensus-driven management styles that are win-win; whereas men are motivated by competition, are willing to elbow others aside to get ahead, and often don't see the point if there isn't a clear winner and loser.[14]

It is scientifically proven that women are not impressed by and do not value physical risk, yet men are more likely to engage in dangerous behavior and more likely to describe dangerous activity as "exhilarating."[15]

When Robert Johnson, president of the Institute for New Economic Thinking, was asked at a conference if he could do one thing to improve the financial system, his answer was simple: "Only allow women to regulate finance."[16]

The audience laughed, but he wasn't joking. Research shows men choose risk even when logic dictates against it, while women choose security even when the risks are low.[17]

Considering all of the above, you can see why things like speculative finance, going to war, and plundering the planet for profit are subliminally attractive to men—yet women are rarely inclined to allow the lure of risk, danger, or competition to influence their decisions. In fact, when thinking sad thoughts, women's brains are eight times more active than men's—making women significantly more empathetic to others around them, less keen to harm, and more eager to help.[18]

In her fabulous book, *Wonder Women*, Debora Spar says we need to stop wishing away biological differences and start analyzing them:

> It's not clear (at least to me) why being supportive of women's ambition means denying the possibility of biologically driven implications. Are all women, under all circumstances, predestined to behave in certain ways or perform certain functions? Of course not. But are women, in general, more or less likely to evince particular characteristics? Maybe. And if those characteristics can be usefully harnessed—if they can, in fact, help us to define models of work and leadership that might fit more comfortably around women—then they almost certainly demand some measure of scrutiny.[19]

It's no coincidence that women are five times more likely to hold the role of CEO within a charity foundation than within the corporate world.[20] Overall, nonprofits are more responsive to human needs in their decision making, more conscious of the ripple effects of their actions, and less motivated by profit as their primary measure of success—all factors which make them more conducive to female leadership.

Yet the majority of businesses and organizations out there are not conducive. And rather than constantly expecting women to adapt to the toxic, masculine-minded environments that already exist, we must focus on creating cultures within all companies that recognize, utilize, and maximize female strengths on all levels.

There's no question it would better for women.

But it would also be a great deal better for the world.

OUR ONCE UPON A TIME IS NOW

. . .

At a certain point, it's not enough for women to have the audacity of hope, or even the audacity of activism. We need the audacity to wield our power.

– MARIANNE WILLIAMSON

FOR THE LAST FIVE hundred years, our world has been largely defined by men and their competitive, production-oriented, financially dominated approach. Unfortunately for all of us, respect for the planet and the well-being of those on it have not been top priorities.

With so much of our world in freefall, some predict that feminine thinking is actually destined to become the modus operandi of the twenty-first century. This means that embracing your inner princess is not just something you will do at the spa; it is something that will eventually give you a competitive advantage. Suddenly empathy will mean innovation; suddenly vulnerability will mean strength.

In this context, the idea of a princess is not regressive but a *breakthrough*. Because it will actually be *the most advanced and progressive* among us who will break away from the status quo and become more feminine on all fronts. I agree that no human quality belongs entirely to one gender, but the skills required to survive in the next few decades happen to come more naturally to women. The question is which women will continue to stifle those qualities and which women will choose to leverage them for the greater good.

"Masculine power has been driving us for thousands of years," says executive coach and author Lisa Marie Jenkins. "But feminine energy is being called upon now for the next stage of human evolution and will be a requirement to transform our world." The feminists of the future will be advocating ideas of "healing, creating balance, and fostering peace."[21]

It's increasingly clear that, male or female, effective leaders of the future will require a much larger dose of emotional and social intelligence—this means more communication, more empathy, and more humility. This means less risk, less aggression, less winner-takes-all competition. This means caring more about humanitarian bottom lines and less about financial ones. This means, instead of being forced to choose between power and warmth, we will *combine* them.

Credit Suisse examined almost 2,400 global corporations and found that companies with at least one woman on their board outperformed comparable companies with all-male boards by 26 percent.[22] Another study found that boards with high female representation experience a 53 percent higher return on equity, a 66 percent higher return on invested capital, and a 42 percent higher return on sales. And having just one female director on the board cuts the risk of bankruptcy by 20 percent.[23]

But there is more than just a business case for feminine thinking. There is a global case as well.

According to authors of *The Athena Doctrine: How Women (and the Men Who Think Like Them) Will Rule the Future*, "We live in a world that is increasingly social, interdependent and transparent. And in this world, feminine values are ascendant."[24]

Allow me to point out that Athena is the goddess of wisdom, courage, and justice, revered for her intelligence, diplomacy, and fairness. When conflicts arise, she responds with tactical communication (unlike her brother Ares, who automatically resorts to violence). But she is also the daughter of Zeus, King of the Greek gods—which makes her a princess. Coincidence? I think not.

(I find it interesting that women never balk when the term "goddess" is used to describe feminine empowerment, while the word "princess" is still questioned. Yet most mythical goddesses are also princesses!)

Drawing from interviews in eighteen nations, *The Athena Doctrine* reveals how both men and women are recognizing significant value in traditionally feminine traits such as patience, collaboration, intuition, flexibility, loyalty, expressiveness, and long-term planning.

In their survey, participants were asked whether they thought the world would be a better place if men thought more like women and 66 percent agreed. Their data further revealed that countries whose citizens think in a more feminine way have a higher per capita GDP and a higher quality of life.

The idea of a princess—the most ancient symbol of feminine power—is re-emerging so intensely in the hearts and minds of women of all ages because our world is screaming out for more feminine thinking.

"Women have always been agents of change," said the first female Speaker of the House, Nancy Pelosi. "They are what I like to call 'magnificent disrupters.' They are unsatisfied with the status quo, and always demanding progress—on behalf of their children, their families and their communities."[25]

Research from the Bill and Melinda Gates Foundation shows that women invest more of their earnings than men do in their family's well-being—as much as ten times more. They prioritize things like health care, nutritious food, and education. In the developing world, when a mother controls her family's budget, her children are 20 percent more likely to survive.[26]

Author Marianne Williamson, founder of women's think tank Sister Giant, talks about how many believe our grandmothers were wrong to see the care of home and children as a woman's highest calling. But the truth is that they had it more than right. We just need to widen the definition and understand that the *whole planet* is our home and *every single child on it* is one of our children. We would never let anyone enter our homes and endanger our own children; yet time and time again we allow aggression and greed to endanger children all over the world.

Williamson reminds us that,

A common anthropological characteristic of all advanced mammalian species is the fierce behavior of the adult female when she senses a threat to her cubs. From the lioness to the tigress to the mama bear, any threat to her cubs is met with a ferocious response. Female hyenas encircle their cubs while they're feeding, not letting the adult males get anywhere near the food, until the babies have been fed. Surely the women of America can do better than the hyenas.[27]

She has a point. More than 23 percent of American children live in poverty. According to the UN Children's Fund, when it comes to relative child poverty, the United States ranks 34th out of the top 35 developed countries—only slightly better than Romania.[28] There is no excuse for this.

Women don't have to have physically given birth to know that we are the mothers of the world and the matriarchs of our kingdoms. Women have a royal duty to speak out on behalf of our planet, our children, and for the millions of women who cannot speak for themselves. Women need to stop obsessing about getting more power and start using the tremendous feminine powers that we already have—and have kept hidden for far too long.

This is why little girls across the globe are so entranced by *Frozen*'s Queen Elsa. Elsa doesn't hide her femininity, and she certainly doesn't hide her inherent magic. Her natural power scares her at first, and it takes her a while to get it right, but when she does, her entire kingdom prospers.

"We need more than a new politics," says Williamson, "We need a new worldview. We need to shift from an economic organizing principle to a humanitarian one. And women, en masse, should be saying so."[29]

Our little girls are *already* saying so. How else could 25,000 princess products be selling so easily and at such voracious speed? Girls are unconsciously demanding a feminine takeover. They don't want to do things the old way; they want princess power, with all its feminine ferocity, to be the new status quo.

And rightly so.

Of course there are those who will continue to pick fights with me about what feminine thinking means for our future. They will argue that "girls should be encouraged to be architects or firemen or senators—*not* princesses!"

These people are far too literal.

Because all work begins with the princess inside of you. "The princess" is merely a reflection of your feminine character—how you treat others, how you work with people, whether you have integrity. No matter what the circumstances of your job, will you have the strength of will to consider the global and human implications of your decisions, not just the financial ones? Will you do your utmost to seek win-win solutions for all concerned? Will you take responsibility for others' well-being and empower others to do the same?

When you access your inner princess, you go about your life with grace, benevolence, and the quiet confidence of a true leader. You wear your invisible crown, and, just like a child, you refuse to take it off. When you access your inner princess, you access your highest self.

It is not an exaggeration to say that we are living in a convergence of economic, environmental, and humanitarian crises. With our planet in turmoil on every level, now is not the time to disregard the power of the princess. Now is the time to claim it.

By doing this, we may be labeled weak, silly, and regressive. We may be accused of sending women back into the dark ages or at least back into the kitchen. But, as women, we know that a more compassionate and collaborative society is possible—and the only way toward a more sustainable future. So we must keep our eyes on the throne.

There cannot be too many princesses.

There cannot be too many queens.

Our once upon a time is *now*.

Epilogue:

HAPPILY EVER AFTER?

· · · · ·

I T WAS BOUND TO happen.

The dreamy English boyfriend and I got engaged. It wasn't how I'd pictured it as a little girl. He didn't ride up to me on a white horse in the middle of an enchanted forest, but he did kneel at my feet in our London flat. And you know what? Despite the rather conventional setting, I still heard Disney music in my head—and, like all heroines, that's how I knew that it was right.

We didn't get married on a tropical beach, and, unlike my parents, we certainly didn't get married standing in a yin yang of flower petals with drops of LSD in the punchbowl. Instead, we decided to celebrate our nuptials at Hampton Court Palace, former residence of King Henry VIII. (And if my recent past-life readings were to be believed, possibly a former residence of mine as well.)

Much to my relief, my hippie father, with his beard and long braided hair, agreed to wear a tailcoat as he walked me down the aisle. And I hardly need to tell you that I wore a tiara and a white satin ball gown with a giant poofy skirt.

So there I was in the Great Hall of Hampton Court with its enormous vaulted ceilings, gazing out at my candlelit banquet of wedding guests: family from Colorado, old friends from college, and new friends from London. The Queen was not in attendance—something that as a child I'd always hoped for—but, oddly enough, it didn't matter. Because as I feasted in the same spot Henry VIII had done five hundred years ago, I knew that generations of Tudors and Stuarts and Hanovers were there with me. It wasn't like I was seeing royal ghosts left and right, but, quite unmistakably, I could feel their ancient presence. And knowing I had a royal family with me that day (albeit a celestial one) certainly added to my happiness.

I caught the eye of my own handsome prince, who was now my husband, and my heart pounded. My life hadn't happened *at all* how I'd planned it. Not even close. But, nevertheless, my girlhood dream of a "royal" wedding *had* come true. And my personal Prince Charming was better than anything Disney could conjure.

But was it the best day of my life? The blissful fairytale culmination marking the end of my life's work as a woman? Of course not.

It was a crazy day, sometimes a stressful day, a hilarious day, and, being in England, it eventually became quite a rainy day.

Earlier that morning, my new husband and I posed for wedding photos in Hampton Court's beautifully manicured gardens. The palace was open to the public, so there were a few families touring the grounds. As I maneuvered my giant wedding dress around the terraced flower beds and animal-shaped topiaries, I noticed a little girl, no more than three years old, standing near the garden gates.

As I walked deeper into the garden to pose near the fountain, I heard the little girl whisper, "Look, Mummy—it's a *princess!*"

I stopped dead in my tracks. At last it had happened. At last, after all these years, someone had recognized me.

I winked at the little girl, and she smiled at me as if we were sharing a secret.

I wanted to tell her that it takes one to know one. But I didn't have to. She knew.

The princess in her had seen the princess in me.

Did I live happily ever after?

Let's just say that if I've learned anything in this life, it's that "happily ever after" is a state of mind you have to create—every day, every moment—for yourself. And when all princesses realize that? Our power will rewrite fairy tales forevermore.

SPECIAL THANKS

· · · · ·

To Aubrey Arnason and Sarah Groundwater-Law, who have been my regal cheerleaders from the start; and to Sophia Holeman, Laurel Issen, Amy Gray, Katherine Longhi, and Olivia Vandyk, who volunteered to read countless drafts and offered so much valuable insight—you are true princesses, one and all.

To Marianne Williamson and Justine Musk—two royal goddesses who inspire me with their words and wisdom every single day. I urge everyone to follow their work.

To my loyal agent, Laura Langlie, who has always understood the true meaning of princess power.

To my noble editors: Sophia Muthuraj (of Grace Kelly Drive), for taking a chance on me and for freely admitting that she loves Princess Diana; and Jennifer Kasius, for recognizing my inner debutante, for getting my Anglophilia, and for transforming this book into something more than accidentally smart.

To my always-chivalrous husband, who is slowly but surely learning to tell the Disney princesses apart.

And to my parents, who have honored my sovereignty from the very, very beginning.

NOTES

· · · · ·

I IN DEFENSE OF DISNEY PRINCESSES

1. Beverley Turner, "I'd Happily Blow the Brains Out of a Disney Princess," *Telegraph*, November 11, 2013.
2. Amy M. Davis, *Good Girls and Wicked Witches* (John Libbey, 2006).
3. Peggy Orenstein, *Cinderella Ate My Daughter* (HarperCollins, 2011).
4. Virginia Woolf, "Professions for Women," in *Collected Essays* (Hogarth Press, 1966).
5. Rachel Simmons, *The Curse of the Good Girl* (Penguin, 2009).
6. Neil Gaiman, "Happily Ever After," *Guardian*, October 13, 2007.
7. Jack Zipes, *Why Fairy Tales Stick: The Evolution and Relevance of a Genre* (Routledge, 2006).
8. Marina Warner, *Once Upon a Time* (Oxford University Press, 2014).
9. Bruno Bettleheim, *The Uses of Enchantment: The Meaning and Importance of Fairy Tales* (Knopf, 1976).
10. Erica Jong, *How to Save Your Own Life*, (1977).
11. justinemusk.com
12. http://princessfreezone.com/.
13. http://www.megcabot.com/2010/12/the-princess-thing/.

14. Sam Keen, *To Love and Be Loved* (Bantam, 1999).

15. @emwatson on Twitter.

16. On the deluxe *Frozen* CD, you will find a song called "We Know Better," which sadly was cut from the final film. The song is about little Princess Anna and little Princess Elsa bonding over the things the world expects and thinks of them because of their royal titles, and it directly counteracts many of the prevailing myths about princesses. It's a fantastic song with a great message, and it's a real shame it didn't make it onto the big screen.

17. Binyamin Appelbaum, "How Disney Turned *Frozen* Into a Cash Cow," *New York Times*, November 18, 2014.

18. Joan Gould, *Spinning Straw into Gold* (Random House, 2005).

19. Ibid.

20. Maureen Murdock, interview cited in *The Heroine's Journey* (Shambhala, 1990).

21. Orenstein, *Cinderella Ate My Daughter*.

22. http://justinemusk.com/.

23. Naomi Wolf, "Mommy, I Want to Be a Princess." *New York Times*, December 2, 2011.

II IN DEFENSE OF PRINCESS PLAY

1. Marianne Williamson, *A Return to Love: Reflections on the Principles of* A Course in Miracles (HarperCollins, 1992).

2. David Auerbach, "The Princess Trap," *Slate*, December 2, 2014.

3. http://www.lizburns.org/2014/12/princess-shaming.html.
4. http://www.skepticalob.com/2014/12/in-praise-of-princesses .html.
5. Frances Hodgson Burnett, *A Little Princess* (Scribner, 1905).
6. Sharon Hayes and Stacey Tantleff-Dunn, "Am I Too Fat to Be a Princess? Examining the Effects of Popular Children's Media on Young Girls' Body Image," *British Journal of Developmental Psychology* 28, no. 2 (June 2010): 413–426.
7. Naomi Wolf, *The Beauty Myth* (Bantham, 1991).
8. Naomi Wolf, "Mommy, I Want to Be a Princess," *New York Times*, December 2011.
9. Yael Kohen, "What's the Problem with Pink, Anyway?," *New York,* March 27, 2014.
10. Susan Wloszczyna, "A Fairy-Tale Bending," *USA Today*, September 17, 2003.
11. Karen Wohlwend, "Damsels in Discourse: Girls Consuming and Producing Identity Texts Through Disney Princess Play," *Reading Research Quarterly* 44 (2009).
12. Kennedy Bailey, "Disney Princesses Have Mixed Effects on Children," *Digital Universe*, Brigham Young University, September 20, 2013.
13. Michael Gurian, *The Wonder of Girls: Understanding the Hidden Nature of Our Daughters* (Atria, 2002).
14. Kohen, "What's the Problem with Pink, Anyway?"
15. Allison Benedikt, "The Problem with Your Problem with Pink," *Slate,* March 28, 2014.
16. princess-awesome.com.
17. Carrie Seim, "Are Tiaras the New Power Scrunchies?," *New York Times*, December 3, 2014.

18. Official White House Photo by Pete Souza. May 27, 2014.

19. Hayley Krischer, "I'm a Feminist Mom—and My Daughter Loves Princesses," *Huffington Post*, November 20, 2011.

20. William Martson, *American Scholar* 13 (1943): 35–44.

21. Jill Lepore, "The Last Amazon," *New Yorker*, September 22, 2014.

22. Noah Berlatsky, "Toward a More Expansive Definition of Princess," *Atlantic*, May 21, 2013.

23. Eric Luke and Joanna Sandsmark, *Wonder Woman: Secret Files and Origins* 1, no. 2, DC Comics, July 1999.

24. Lepore, "Last Amazon."

25. Jill Lepore, *The Secret History of Wonder Woman* (Knopf, 2014).

26. Hilary Whiteman, "Diane von Furstenberg, the Wonder Woman," CNN, November 7, 2008.

27. Ally Pyle, "DVF Wonder Woman," *Vogue*, July 2008.

III IN DEFENSE OF PINK AND GIRLY

1. Amy Morin, "How to Use Color Psychology to Give Your Business an Edge," *Forbes*, February 4, 2014.

2. Commissioned by Cotton USA in 2012.

3. http://www.remodelista.com.

4. Priya Elan, "Think Pink: How the Colour Is Being Reclaimed," *Guardian*, September 10, 2014.

5. Rebecca Hains, *The Princess Problem* (Sourcebooks, 2014).

6. Jo Paoletti, *Pink and Blue: Telling the Boys from the Girls in America* (University of Utah Press, 2010).

7. Polly Vernon, *Hot Feminist* (Hodder & Stoughton, 2015).

8. Alice Dreger, "The Social Construction of Sex," *Pacific Standard*, March 21, 2014.

9. Laura Hudson, "Toy Company Wants to Turn Princesses into Engineers," *Wired*, April 9, 2014.

10. Melanie Nelson, "So What If My Girls Are Princesses?" *USA Today*, December 2014.

IV IN DEFENSE OF THE PRINCESS ARCHETYPE

1. Virginia Postrel, "Still Gripped by the Ideal of the Princess," *Wall Street Journal*, December 18, 2010.

2. Tina Brown, *The Diana Chronicles* (Doubleday, 2007).

3. Hilary Mantel, "Royal Bodies," *London Review of Books* 35, no. 4 (February 21, 2013).

4. Naomi Wolf, "From Lady Di to Michelle Obama," *Project Syndicate*, March 2009.

5. Monica Ali, "Royal Rebel: The Legacy of Diana," *Guardian*, March 30, 2011.

6. *People*, October 2014.

7. Anthony Lane, "Hollywood Royalty: The Two Sides of Grace Kelly," *New Yorker*, January 2010.

8. Brown, *Diana Chronicles*.

9. Robert McFadden, "Death of a First Lady," *New York Times*, May 20, 1994.

10. Ibid.

11. When Catherine married Prince William, she became Princess William of Wales and would have retained this title if William had not received a dukedom as a wedding gift from the Queen.

V IN DEFENSE OF BEAUTY

1. http://justinemusk.com/.

2. Bob McLain, "Peggy Orenstein, Cinderella Ate My Daughter: Bob Chats with Peggy about Disney's Appetite for Little Girls" (interview), February 3, 2011, DisneyDispatch.com.

3. Faran Krentcil, "How Disney Princess Culture Helped Me Be a Strong, Smart Girl," *Elle*, May 2014.

4. Cindy Faith Miller, Leah E. Lurye, Kristina M. Zosuls, and Diane N. Ruble, "Accessibility of Gender Stereotype Domains: Developmental and Gender Differences in Children," *Sex Roles* 60, nos. 11–12 (June 2009): 870–881.

5. Dana Benbow, "Experts: Mom Has Biggest Impact on Girls' Body Image," *USA Today*, August 23, 2013.

6. Peggy Orenstein, "What's Wrong with Cinderella?," *New York Times*, December 24, 2006.

7. Justine Musk, "The Art of Thinking Highly of Yourself," *Huffington Post*, July 22, 2013.

8. "New 'Cosmo' Woman Is 'Interested in Mascara and the Middle East,'" *NPR Morning Edition*, October 14, 2014.

9. Charlotte Alter, "In Defense of Barbie: Why She Might Be the Most Feminist Doll Around," *Time*, February 5, 2014.

10. I will concede that no one *ever* talks about what male politicians are wearing. But maybe they should. In the wise words of writer Fran Lebowitz, "If you cover a man's eyes, he legitimately might not remember what he has on. But is that really worth celebrating, or imitating? Personally I don't think we need to emulate that level of stupidity" (*Elle* magazine, March 2015).

11. Debora Spar, *Wonder Women: Sex, Power, and the Quest for Perfection* (Picador, 2013).

12. Elizabeth Gilbert, Facebook.com/GilbertLiz.

VI IN DEFENSE OF REAL ROYAL WOMEN

1. Marlo Thomas, "The Baby King . . . and Why We Care," *Huffington Post*, July 26, 2013.

2. Martin Gilens and Benjamin I. Page, "Testing Theories of American Politics: Elites, Interest Groups, and Average Citizens," *Perspectives on Politics* 12, no. 3 (September 2014).

3. Karen McVeigh, "George P. Bush and the US Obsession with Political Dynasties," *Guardian*, March 11, 2014.

4. Snejana Farberov, "Is Ruling in the Genes?" *Daily Mail*, August 5, 2012. (Only Martin Van Buren was not related to King John.)

5. Satoshi Kanazawa, "Genes for Monarchy?" *Psychology Today*, February 21, 2010.

6. Brown, *Diana Chronicles*.

7. Jeremy Paxman, *On Royalty* (Penguin, 2007).

8. Matthew Dennison, "Elizabeth Is About to Become Britain's Longest-Reigning Queen: Here's How She's Changed Monarchy," *Spectator*, January 3, 2015.

9. Sally Peck, "Why Americans Just Don't Get the Royal Family," *Daily Telegraph*, July 24, 2013.

10. Quoted in Ed Docx, "The Duchess of Cambridge: How Britain Stopped Believing in the Royal Fairytale," *Newsweek*, September 25, 2014.

11. UBN Radio/TV, Singin' in the Rain with Sunny Chayes: Marianne Williamson, October 14, 2015.

12. Michelle Green, "Princess Bride," *People*, January 25, 1993.

13. *Tatler*, December 2010.

14. Translated from Swedish *Elle*, January 2010.

VII IN DEFENSE OF THE PRINCE

1. Lisa Phillips, *Unrequited* (HarperCollins, 2015).

2. Elizabeth Gilbert, *Committed* (Bloomsbury, 2010).

3. Naomi Wolf, *Fire with Fire* (Vintage, 1994).

4. Interview, *BBC News*, January 21, 2013.

VIII IN DEFENSE OF FEMININE POWER (YOUR INNER PRINCESS)

1. Betsey Stevenson and Justin Wolfers, "Economic Growth and Subjective Well-Being: Reassessing the Easterlin Paradox," The National Bureau of Economic Research, Working Paper No. 14282, August 2008.
2. Barbara Annis and Keith Merron, *Gender Intelligence: Breakthrough Strategies for Increasing Diversity and Improving Your Bottom Line* (HarperBusiness, 2014).
3. Marianne Williamson, *A Woman's Worth* (Ballentine, 1993).
4. Polly Vernon, "So What Does a Feminist Look Like?," *Evening Standard Magazine*, May 29, 2015.
5. Wolf, *Fire with Fire*.
6. https://m.facebook.com/GilbertLiz.
7. Julia Serano, *Whipping Girl* (Seal Press, 2007).
8. A review of 127 studies involving 28,000 children by Hugh Lytton and David Romney, "Parents' Differential Socialization of Boys and Girls: A Meta-Analysis," *Psychological Bulletin* 109 (1991): 267–296.
9. Marianne Williamson, "Feminine 2.0," *Huffington Post*, March 8, 2011.
10. Three studies cited by Leonard Sax in *Why Gender Matters* (Three Rivers Press, 2005).
11. Judith Hall, *Non Verbal Sex Differences* (Johns Hopkins University Press, 1985); also Erin McClur, "A Meta Analysis Review of the Sex Differences in Facial Expression Processing," *Psychological Bulletin* 126 (2000): 424–53.

12. "Does Estrogen Make You Smarter?," *New York Magazine*, August 1997.

13. Helen Fisher, *The First Sex: The Natural Talents of Women* (Ballentine, 1999).

14. Ibid.

15. Barbara Morrongiello, "Children's Perspectives on Injury and Close-Call Experiences: Sex Differences in Injury-Outcome Processes," *Journal of Pediatric Psychology* 22, no. 4 (1997). Also Lizette Peterson, Tammy Brazeal, et al. "Gender and Developmental Patterns of Affect, Belief and Behaviours in Simulated Injury Events," *Journal of Applied Developmental Psychology* 18 (1997).

16. William Greider, "What Would Happen If Women Were in Charge of the Global Economy?" *Nation*, May 8, 2015.

17. Muriel Niederle and Lise Vesterlund, "Do Women Shy Away from Competition? Do Men Compete Too Much?," *Quarterly Journal of Economics* 122 (2007).

18. Fisher, *First Sex*.

19. Debora Spar, *Wonder Women: Sex, Power, and the Quest for Perfection* (Picador, 2013).

20. Council on Foundations, 1998.

21. Lisa Marie Jenkins, "What's So Feminine about Being a Feminist?," *Huffington Post*, November 25, 2014.

22. Therese Huston, "Are Women Better Decision Makers?," *New York Times*, October 17, 2014.

23. Chris Bart and Gregory McQueen, "Why Women Make Better Directors," *International Journal of Business Governance and Ethics* 8 (2013).

24. Michael D'Antonio and John Gerzema, *The Athena Doctrine* (Jossey-Bass, 2013).

25. Marianne Schnall, "Reflections on Occupy Wall Street," *Huffington Post,* January 5, 2012.

26. Melinda Gates, "Why Development Begins with Women," *Impatient Optimists,* October 12, 2014, Bill & Melinda Gates Foundation.

27. Williamson, "Feminine 2.0."

28. Max Fisher, "Map: How 35 Countries Compare on Child Poverty (the U.S. Is Ranked 34th)," *Washington Post,* April 15, 2013.

29. Marianne Williamson, "Women, Non-Violence and Birthing a New American Politics," Sistergiant.com.

PERMISSIONS

. . .

ABOUT THE AUTHOR

. . . . .

J ERRAMY FINE WAS RAISED IN rural Colorado, where her hippie parents hoped and prayed she would outgrow her princess obsession. But she never did. Instead, she moved to England to seek out a more royal life. Her childhood quest to become a princess is detailed in her hilarious memoir *Someday My Prince Will Come*. Fine studied political science at the University of Rochester and social science at the London School of Economics. She has appeared in defense of the princess on *The Today Show, CNN, CBS News, BBC World,* and *Inside Edition,* among others, and as a royal expert for the *Daily Beast, Newsweek, InTouch, Closer,* and *Life & Style* magazines. She lives in London with her British husband, a three-year-old princess, and a giant golden retriever.

www.jerramyfine.com
@missjfine